I0019979

Practical Electronics

Volume I

8085 Microprocessor & 8051 Microcontroller Laboratory Manual

T. VEERAMANIKANDASAMY

Assistant Professor
Department of Electronics and Communication Systems
Sri Krishna Arts and Science College
Coimbatore – 641008, India

A. BALAMURUGAN

Assistant Professor
Department of Physics
Government Arts and Science College
Avinashi – 641654, India

Practical Electronics

Volume I

8085 Microprocessor & 8051 Microcontroller Laboratory Manual

Copyright © 2019 T.Veeramanikandasamy

ISBN: **9781651706701** (Paperback)

Cover image by T.Veeramanikandasamy

First Edition 2019

About the Authors

Dr. T. Veeramanikandasamy is an Assistant Professor of Electronics and Communication Systems at Sri Krishna Arts and Science College, Coimbatore 641 008. He obtained his Doctorate in Electronics from Bharathiar University, Coimbatore, India. He has 13 years of teaching experience. His current research interests are in Nanomaterials Characterization, Embedded Systems, and Digital Signal Processing. Five candidates were awarded the M.Phil degree under his guidance. He has published two books with ISBN. He has published 11 research papers in peer-reviewed international journals. He has presented more than sixteen research papers in national/international conferences. He has delivered more than ten technical lectures in various institutions. He is a Life Member of the Indian Society of Systems for Science and Engineering (ISSE). He holds a certification in Embedded Software Engineer (NSQF-QP ELE/Q1501) received from the Electronics Sector Skills Council of India. He has developed various student enrichment courses on Embedded Systems, Digital System Design, Digital Signal Processing, Programmable Logic Controller, and IoT with Python.

Dr. A. Balamurugan has 20 years of teaching experience at the undergraduate and postgraduate levels. He has obtained a Doctorate degree from Bharathiar University, Coimbatore, Tamilnadu, India. His fields of specialization include experimental nonlinear systems and nanomaterials. Under his supervision, five students were awarded Ph.D. and six students were awarded M.Phil degree. Currently, he is working as Professor and Head, Department of Physics, Government Arts and Science College, Avinashi, Tamilnadu, India. He also served on various committees of academic matter appointed by the State and Central Government. He has published more than thirty papers in national and international journals. He has presented more than sixty research articles in conferences. He has authored three books and acted as editor for publishing books. He has received the Best Researcher award.

PREFACE

Laboratory experiences are the part of science and technology curricula of higher education. This laboratory manual intended to support the undergraduate and postgraduate students in the related fields of Electronics for practicing embedded system experiments. The chapters begin with an introduction, and it covers the experiments for the 8085 Microprocessor & 8051 Microcontroller laboratory. Each experiment consists of aim, hardware/software requirements, algorithm, program, experimental results, and conclusion. For the most part, the lab manual includes the standard laboratory experiments that have been used by many academicians related to electronics departments for years. Over sixty-three practical experiments described here to explore the practical knowledge of students on embedded systems. This book comprises two chapters that are focused on the lab experiments of the 8085 Microprocessor & 8051 Microcontroller laboratory.

This book helps to

- Promote experiential learning among the students
- Give practical or informal knowledge to understand how things work
- Know the interaction between software and hardware

Please contact me at veeramaniks@gmail.com if you find any errors or have any suggestions for improvements in the laboratory manual. I will incorporate your suggestions and rectify the errors in the next edition.

- **Dr. T. Veeramanikandasamy**

CONTENTS

2   8051 Microcontroller Laboratory

Chapter - 1

8085 MICROPROCESSOR LABORATORY

1.1 Introduction to 8085 Microprocessor

The microprocessor is a semiconductor device built on a chip manufactured by the Very Large Scale Integration (VLSI) technology. It includes the Arithmetic and Logic Unit (ALU), Register array, Timing, and control unit, an Instruction register and Instruction decoder to perform the task defined by the user program. It enclosed with 40-pins and requires +5V supply to operate at 3.2 MHz single-phase clock. It can be connected with peripherals like memory, an input device, an output device, and interfacing devices.

The 8085 is an 8-bit microprocessor, and it was launched by Intel in the year of 1976 with the help of NMOS technology. The data bus carries data, in binary form, between a microprocessor and other peripheral units. The typical size of the data bus is 8 bits (AD_0-AD_7). The 8085 has a 16-bit address bus and can address up to 65536 bytes (64 KB) through address lines AD_0-AD_7 and A_8-A_{15}.

The general-purpose 8-bit registers are Accumulator (A), B, C, D, E,

1

H, & L. The permitted couples are BC, DE & HL with 16-bit storage capacity. The special purposes registers are program counter (16), the stack pointer (16), increment or decrement register (16/8), address buffer and data buffer.

The timing and control unit provides/receives the following signals to perform operations,

- Status Signals: S0, S1, IO/M'
- Control Signals: READY, RD', WR', ALE
- DMA Signals: HOLD, HLDA
- RESET Signals: RESET IN, RESET OUT

An instruction is a binary code used to perform a specific function in a microprocessor and a microcontroller. The entire group of instructions or instruction set of 8085 microprocessor is classified into the following five functional categories:

1. **Data Transfer Group instructions** load the data into the register, move data from the register to register, and move data from register to memory location and vice versa.

2. **Arithmetic Group instructions** perform basic arithmetic operations. The destination operand is generally the accumulator.

3. **Logical Group instructions** perform basic logical operations.

4. **Branch Control Group instructions** allow the microprocessor to change the sequence of a program.

5. **I/O and Machine Control Group instructions** perform input/output ports, stack, and machine control operations.

Data Transfer Group

Move

MOV			MOV			MOV		
A,A	7F		B,A	47		C,A	4F	
A,B	78		B,B	40		C,B	48	
A,C	79		B,C	41		C,C	49	
A,D	7A		B,D	42		C,D	4A	
A,E	7B		B,E	43		C,E	4B	
A,H	7C		B,H	44		C,H	4C	
A,L	7D		B,L	45		C,L	4D	
A,M	7E		B,M	46		C,M	4E	

MOV			MOV			MOV		
D,A	57		E,A	5F		H,A	67	
D,B	50		E,B	58		H,B	60	
D,C	51		E,C	59		H,C	61	
D,D	52		E,D	5A		H,D	62	
D,E	53		E,E	5B		H,E	63	
D,H	54		E,H	5C		H,H	64	
D,L	55		E,L	5D		H,L	65	
D,M	56		E,M	5E		H,M	66	

Move Immediate

MOV			MOV			MVI		
L,A	6F		M,A	77		A,byte	3E	
L,B	68		M,B	70		B,byte	06	
L,C	69		M,C	71		C,byte	0E	
L,D	6A		M,D	72		D,byte	16	
L,E	6B		M,E	73		E,byte	1E	
L,H	6C		M,H	74		H,byte	26	
L,L	6D		M,L	75		L,byte	2E	
L,M	6E					M,byte	36	

Load Immediate (Reg. pair)

LXI		
B,dble	01	
D,dble	11	
H,dble	21	
SP,dble	31	

Load/Store A direct

LDAX B	0A
LDAX D	1A
STAX B	02
STAX D	12

Load/Store A direct

LDA addr	3A
STA addr	32

Load/Store HL direct

LHLD addr	2A
SHLD addr	22

Exchange HL with DE

XCHG	EB

3

Arithmetic Group

Add

ADD		
	A	87
	B	80
	C	81
	D	82
	E	83
	H	84
	L	85
	M	86

ADC		
	A	8F
	B	88
	C	89
	D	8A
	E	8B
	H	8C
	L	8D
	M	8E

Increment/Decrement

INR		
	A	3C
	B	04
	C	0C
	D	14
	E	1C
	H	24
	L	2C
	M	34

Subtract

SUB		
	A	97
	B	90
	C	91
	D	92
	E	93
	H	94
	L	95
	M	96

SBB		
	A	9F
	B	98
	C	99
	D	9A
	E	9B
	H	9C
	L	9D
	M	9E

DCR		
	A	3D
	B	05
	C	0D
	D	15
	E	1D
	H	25
	L	2D
	M	35

Add/Subtract Immediate

ADI byte	C6
ACI byte	CE
SUI byte	D6
SBI byte	DE

Increment/Decrement Register Pair

INX		
	B	03
	D	13
	H	23
	SP	33

DCX		
	B	0B
	D	1B
	H	2B
	SP	3B

Double Length Add

DAD		
	B	09
	D	19
	H	29
	SP	39

Decimal Adjust A

DAA	27

Complement/Set CY

CMC	3F
STC	37

Complement A

CMA	2F

Arithmetic Immediate

ADI byte	C6
ACI byte	CE
SUI byte	D6
SBI byte	DE

4

Logical Group

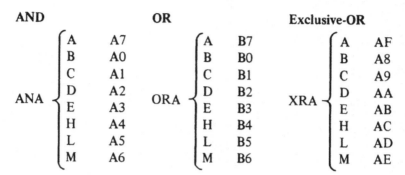

AND

ANA
A	A7
B	A0
C	A1
D	A2
E	A3
H	A4
L	A5
M	A6

OR

ORA
A	B7
B	B0
C	B1
D	B2
E	B3
H	B4
L	B5
M	B6

Exclusive-OR

XRA
A	AF
B	A8
C	A9
D	AA
E	AB
H	AC
L	AD
M	AE

Compare

CMP
A	BF
B	B8
C	B9
D	BA
E	BB
H	BC
L	BD
M	BE

Rotate

RLC	07
RRC	0F
RAL	17
RAR	1F

Logical Immediate

ANI byte	E6
XRI byte	EE
ORI byte	F6
CPI byte	FE

Branch Control Group

Jump		Call		Return	
JMP addr	C3	CALL addr	CD	RET	C9
JNZ addr	C2	CNZ addr	C4	RNZ	C0
JZ addr	CA	CZ addr	CC	RZ	C8
JNC addr	D2	CNC addr	D4	RNC	D0
JC addr	DA	CC addr	DC	RC	D8
JPO addr	E2	CPO addr	E4	RPO	E0
JPE addr	EA	CPE addr	EC	RPE	E8
JP addr	F2	CP addr	F4	RP	F0
JM addr	FA	CM addr	FC	RM	F8

Jump Indirect

PCHL	E9

I/O and Machine Control Group

Input/Output Group

IN port	DB
OUT port	D3

Stack operations

PUSH	B	C5	POP	B	C1
	D	D5		D	D1
	H	E5		H	E1
	PSW	F5		PSW	F1
XTHL	E3		SPHL	F9	

Interrupt Control

EI	FB
DI	F3
RIM	20
SIM	30

Restart

RST		
	0	C7
	1	CF
	2	D7
	3	DF
	4	E7
	5	EF
	6	F7
	7	FF

Processor Control

NOP	00
HLT	76

1.2 Programmable Peripheral Interface - 8255A

The Intel 8255A is a general-purpose programmable I/O device that is designed to use with all Intel and other microprocessors. The 8255 is a 40 pin integrated circuit. It provides 24 I/O pins which may be individually programmed in 2 groups of 12 and used in 3 major modes of operation. The device has three 8-bit ports which are port A, port B and port C. Figure 1.1 shows the pin configuration of 8255A.

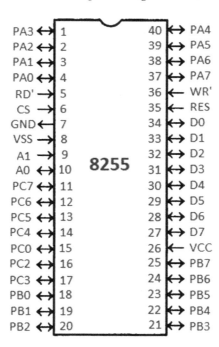

Figure1.1. 8255A Pin Configuration

o   Vcc - +5 volts to this pin

o   GND - Ground this pin

o   CS (chip select) – An active low signal to select this chip.

o   RD (read) – An active low signal to read data from specified port of 8255A.

o   WR (write) - An active low signal to write data on a specified 8255A ports.

o   RESET - A high on this pin will clear all registers and ports.

o   A0 and A1 - These pins select the port A, port B, port C, and control word registers.

There are three modes of operation in 8255A,

o   Mode 0 (Mostly used)

o   Mode 1

o   Mode 2

Mode 0 is a simple input/output mode. Port A, port B, and port C can be used as input or output. Port C can be divided into two nibbles upper and lower.   Both upper and lower can be programmed independently. Figure 1.2 is the control word format of 8255A.

In mode 0, D7 is always '1'. If we select all ports as output ports, the control word will be b'1000 000 (0x80 in hexadecimal).

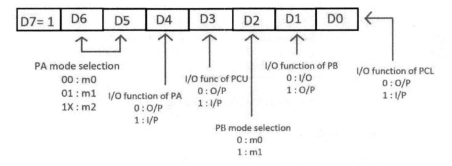

Figure 1.2. Control Word Format of 8255A

1.3	ADDITION OF TWO 8-BIT NUMBERS

Aim:

Write an 8085 assembly language program to perform the addition of two 8-bit numbers.

Apparatus:

- 8085 Microprocessor Trainer

Algorithm:

1. Initialize the memory location of the first operand in HL register pair, HL points 5000H
2. Clear the carry register (C register)
3. Move the first operand into the accumulator (A register)
4. Increment the HL register pair to point out the second operand, HL points 5001H
4. Add the second operand with the accumulator
5. Check whether the carry is generated from the accumulator or not
6. If yes, increments the carry register otherwise skip incrementing carry block
7. Store the sum in memory location 5005H and carry in 5006H

Program:

Memory address	Machine Codes	Mnemonics & Operand(s)	Comments
4000	21		Address of first operand in H-L register pair
4001	00	LXI H, 5000H	
4002	50		
4003	0E	MVI C, 00H	Clear carry register C.
4004	00		
4005	7E	MOV A, M	Get first operand in the accumulator
4006	23	INX H	Increment H-L pair

4007	86	ADD M	Add the second operand with first operand
4008	D2	JNC **400CH**	Jumps to the address 400CH if carry flag is 0.
4009	0C		
400A	40		
400B	0C	INR C	Increment carry register
400C	32	STA 5005H	Store sum in 5005H
400D	05		
400E	50		
400F	79	MOV A, C	Move carry to the Accumulator
4010	32	STA 5006H	Store carry in 5006H
4011	06		
4012	50		
4013	76	HLT	Terminate program execution

Experimental Results:

Input Data		Result	
Memory location	Operand	Memory location	Operand
5000	85 H	5005	2B H (sum)
5001	A6 H	5006	01 H (carry)

Calculation:

I/O	in HEX		in Binary	
Operand 1	85 H		1000	0101
Operand 2	A6 H		1010	0110
Result (carry & sum)	12B H	1	0010	1011

Conclusion:

The addition of two 8-bit numbers is performed using 8085 microprocessor.

1.4	SUBTRACTION OF TWO 8-BIT NUMBERS

Aim:

Write an 8085 assembly language program to perform the subtraction of two 8-bit numbers.

Apparatus:

- o   8085 Microprocessor Trainer

Algorithm:

1. Initialize the memory location of the first operand in HL register pair, HL points 5000H
2. Clear the borrow register (B register)
3. Move the first operand into the accumulator (A register)
4. Increment the HL register pair to point out the second operand, HL points 5001H
4. Subtract the second operand from the accumulator (A<=A-X)
5. Check whether borrow (Carry flag) is generated from the accumulator or not
6. If yes, increments the borrow register otherwise skip incrementing borrow block
7. Store the difference (as a 2's complement number) in memory location 5005H and borrow in 5006H

Program:

Memory address	Machine Codes	Mnemonics & Operand(s)	Comments
4000	21		Address of first operand in H-L register pair
4001	00	LXI H, 5000H	
4002	50		
4003	06	MVI B, 00H	Clear carry register B.
4004	00		
4005	7E	MOV A, M	Get first operand in the accumulator
4006	23	INX H	Increment H-L pair

11

4007	96	SUB M	Subtract the second operand with first operand (A<=A-M)
4008	D2	JNC **400CH**	Jumps to the address 400CH if carry flag is 0.
4009	0C		
400A	40		
400B	04	INR B	Increment borrow register
400C	32	STA 5005H	Store difference (2's complement) in 5005H
400D	05		
400E	50		
400F	78	MOV A, B	Move borrow to the Accumulator
4010	32	STA 5006H	Store borrow in 5006H
4011	06		
4012	50		
4013	76	HLT	Terminate program execution

Experimental Results:

Input Data		Result	
Memory location	Operand	Memory location	Operand
5000	56 H (minuend)	5005	32 H (difference)
5001	24 H (subtrahend)	5006	00 H (borrow)

Calculation:

I/O	in HEX		in Binary	
Minuend	56 H		0101	0110
Subtrahend	24 H		0010	0100
Result (borrow & difference)	32 H	0	0011	0010

Conclusion:

The subtraction of two 8-bit numbers is performed using 8085 microprocessor.

1.5 | ADDITION OF N 8-BIT NUMBERS IN AN ARRAY

Aim:

Write an 8085 assembly language program to perform the addition of N 8-bit numbers in an array.

Apparatus:

- 8085 Microprocessor Trainer

Algorithm:

1. Clear carry register C
2. Initialize the memory location in H-L register pair for giving input data; H-L points 5000H
3. Move the first data of an array (number of array elements) to B register
4. Decrement B register and increment H-L pair to point out the next data
5. Move the first operand into the accumulator (A register)
6. Increment the H-L register pair to point out the next operand
7. Add the accumulator with the data pointed by H-L pair
8. Check whether the carry is generated from the accumulator or not
9. If yes, increments the carry register otherwise skip incrementing carry block
10. Decrement the value of B register, which is used as a counter
11. If the counter is non-zero value, repeat the steps from 6. Otherwise stores the sum in memory location 5010H and carry in 5011H

Program:

Memory address	Machine Codes	Mnemonics	Comments
4000	0E	MVI C, 00H	Clear carry register C.
4001	00		
4002	21	LXI H, 5000H	Initialize the memory location 5000H in H-L register pair for

4003	00		
4004	50		
4005	46	MOV B, M	Move the number of array elements to B
4006	05	DCR B	Decrement B register
4007	23	INX H	Increment H-L pair
4008	7E	MOV A, M	Get first operand at the accumulator
4009	23	INX H	Increment H-L pair
400A	86	ADD M	Add accumulator with content of memory addressed by H-L
400B	D2	JNC 400FH	Jumps to the address 400FH if carry flag is 0.
400C	0F		
400D	40		
400E	0C	INR C	Increment carry register
400F	05	DCR B	Decrement B register
4010	C2	JNZ 4009H	Repeat block from 4009H until 'B' is zero
4011	09		
4012	40		
4013	32	STA 5010H	Store sum in 5010H
4014	10		
4015	50		
4016	79	MOV A, C	Move carry to the A register
4017	32	STA 5011H	Store carry in 5011H
4018	11		
4019	50		
401A	76	HLT	Terminate program execution

Experimental Results:

Input Data		Result	
Memory location	Operand	Memory location	Operand
5000	04 H*	5010	03 H (sum)
5001	16 H	5011	01 H (carry)

5002	42 H		
5003	73 H		
5004	38 H		

* Number of array elements

Calculation:

I/O	in HEX
Count	04 H
Operand 1	16 H
Operand 2	42 H
Operand 3	73 H
Operand 4	38 H
Result	103 H

Conclusion:

The addition of N 8-bit numbers in an array is performed using 8085 microprocessor.

1.6   ADDITION OF TWO BCD NUMBERS

Aim:

Write an 8085 assembly language program to perform the addition of two BCD numbers.

Apparatus:

o   8085 Microprocessor Trainer

Algorithm:

1. Initialize the memory location of the first operand in HL register pair, HL points 5000H
2. Clear the carry register (C register)
3. Move the first operand into the accumulator (A register)
4. Increment the HL register pair to point out the second operand,

HL points 5001H
4. Add the second operand with the accumulator
5. Convert the accumulator value into a BCD value
6. Check whether the carry is generated from the accumulator or not
7. If yes, increments the carry register otherwise skip incrementing carry block
8. Store the sum in memory location 5005H and carry in 5006H

Program:

Memory address	Machine Codes	Mnemonics & Operand(s)	Comments
4000	21		Address of first operand in H-L register pair
4001	00	LXI H, 5000H	
4002	50		
4003	0E	MVI C, 00H	Clear carry register C.
4004	00		
4005	7E	MOV A, M	Get first operand in the accumulator
4006	23	INX H	Increment H-L pair
4007	86	ADD M	Add the second operand with first operand
4008	27	DAA	Adjust the accumulator value to BCD value
4009	D2		Jumps to the address 400DH if carry flag is 0.
400A	0D	JNC **400DH**	
400B	40		
400C	0C	INR C	Increment carry register
400D	32		Store sum in 5005H
400E	05	STA 5005H	
400F	50		
4010	79	MOV A, C	Move carry to the Accumulator
4011	32	STA 5006H	Store carry in 5006H
4012	06		

4013	50		
4014	76	HLT	Terminate program execution

Experimental Results:

Input Data		Result	
Memory location	Operand	Memory location	Operand
5000	49 H	5005	74 H
5001	25 H	5006	00 H

Calculation:

I/O	in HEX		in Binary		
Operand 1	49 H			0100	1001
Operand 2	25 H			0010	0101
Result	16E H		0	0110	1110
BCD Result				0111	0100

Conclusion:

The addition of two BCD numbers is performed using 8085 microprocessor.

1.7 ADDITION OF TWO 16-BIT NUMBERS

Aim:

Write an 8085 assembly language program to perform the addition of two 16-bit binary numbers.

Apparatus:

o   8085 Microprocessor Trainer

Algorithm:

1.   Copy the content of the memory location pointed by the 16-bit

address into register L, and copy the content of the next memory location into register H. (first operand)

2. Exchange the contents of H-L pair with D-E pair

3. Copy the content of the memory location pointed by the 16-bit address into register L, and copy the content of the next memory location into register H. (second operand)

4. Clear the carry register (C register)

5. Add two 16-bit values using DAD D

6. Check whether the carry is generated or not

7. If yes, increments the carry register otherwise skip incrementing carry block

8. Store the 16-bit sum from the memory location 5010H and carry in 5012H

Program:

Memory address	Machine Codes	Mnemonics & Operand(s)	Comments
4000	2A		
4001	00	LHLD 5000H	Get first 16-bit number in H-L.
4002	50		
4003	EB	XCHG	Exchange the contents of H-L and D-E
4004	2A		
4005	02	LHLD 5002H	Get second 16-bit number in H-L.
4006	50		
4007	0E	MVI C, 00H	Clear carry register C.
4008	00		
4009	19	DAD D	Add the contents of H-L with D-E
400A	D2		
400B	0E	JNC **400EH**	Jumps to the address 400EH if carry flag is 0.
400C	40		
400D	0C	INR C	Increment carry register
400E	22	SHLD 5010H	Store 16-bit sum in 5010H

400F	10		
4010	50		
4011	79	MOV A, C	Move carry to the Accumulator
4012	32		
4013	12	STA 5012H	Store carry in 5012H
4014	50		
4015	76	HLT	Terminate program execution

Experimental Results:

Input Data		Result	
Memory location	Operand	Memory location	Operand
5000	A3 H (LSB)	5010	DF H (LSB)
5001	81 H (MSB)	5011	13 H (MSB)
5002	3C H (LSB)	5012	01 H (carry)
5003	92 H (MSB)	-	-

Calculation:

I/O	in HEX		in Binary			
Operand 1	81A3 H		1000	0001	1010	0011
Operand 2	923C H		1001	0010	0011	1100
Result (C & S)	113DF H	1	0001	0011	1101	1111

Conclusion:

The addition of two 16-bit numbers is performed using 8085 microprocessor.

1.8	SUBTRACTION OF TWO 16-BIT NUMBERS

Aim:

Write an 8085 assembly language program to perform the subtraction of two 16-bit binary numbers.

Apparatus:

- o   8085 Microprocessor Trainer

Algorithm:

1. Copy the content of the memory location pointed by the 16-bit address into register L, and copy the content of the next memory location into register H. (first operand)
2. Exchange the contents of H-L pair with D-E pair
3. Copy the content of the memory location pointed by the 16-bit address into register L, and copy the content of the next memory location into register H. (second operand)
4. Move LSB of the first operand to A register
5. Subtract L register from A register
6. Store the LSB of difference into the memory location 5010H
7. Move MSB of the first operand to A register
8. Subtract H register from A register
9. Store the MSB of difference into the memory location 5011H

Program:

Memory address	Machine Codes	Mnemonics & Operand(s)	Comments
4000	2A		
4001	00	LHLD 5000H	Get first 16-bit number in H-L
4002	50		
4003	EB	XCHG	Exchange the contents of H-L and D-E
4004	2A		
4005	02	LHLD 5002H	Get second 16-bit number in H-L
4006	50		
4007	7B	MOV A, E	Move E register content to A reg.
4008	95	SUB L	Subtract L reg. from the
4009	22	STA 5010H	Store the difference (LSB) in 5010H
400A	10		

400B	50		
400C	79	MOV A, D	Move MSB of first operand to A
400D	9C	SBB H	Subtract H from the accumulator
400E	32		Store the difference (MSB) in 5011H
400F	11	STA 5011H	
4010	50		
4011	76	HLT	Terminate program execution

Experimental Results:

Input Data		Result	
Memory location	Operand	Memory location	Operand
5000	A5 H (LSB)	5010	73 H (LSB)
5001	87 H (MSB)	5011	24 H (MSB)
5002	32 H (LSB)	-	-
5003	63 H (MSB)	-	-

Calculation:

I/O	in HEX		in Binary			
Minuend	87A5 H		1000	0111	1010	0101
Subtrahend	6332 H		0110	0011	0011	0010
Result (Difference)	2473 H		0010	0100	0111	0011

Conclusion:

The subtraction of two 16-bit numbers is performed using 8085 microprocessor.

1.9   MULTIPLICATION OF TWO 8-BIT NUMBERS

Aim:

Write an 8085 assembly language program to perform the multiplication of two 8-bit binary numbers.

Apparatus:

- o   8085 Microprocessor Trainer

Algorithm:

1. Clear carry register C
2. Initialize the memory location in H-L register pair for giving input data; H-L points 5000H
3. Move the multiplicand to B register
4. Increment H-L pair to point out the multiplier
5. Clear the accumulator
6. Add the accumulator and multiplier
7. Check whether the carry is generated from the accumulator or not
8. If yes, increments the carry register otherwise skip incrementing carry block
9. Decrement the value of B register
10. Repeat the steps from 6 until B register having a non-zero value. Otherwise stores the LSB of product into the memory location 5003H and MSB of product into the memory location 5004H

Program:

Memory address	Machine Codes	Mnemonics & Operand(s)	Comments
4000	0E	MVI C, 00H	Clear carry register C.
4001	00		
4002	21	LXI H, 5000H	Initialize the memory location 5000H in H-L register pair for input
4003	00		
4004	50		

4005	46	MOV B, M	Move the multiplicand to B reg.
4006	23	INX H	Increment H-L pair
4007	AF	XRA A	Clear the accumulator
4008	86	ADD M	Add accumulator and multiplier
4009	D2		
400A	0D	JNC **400DH**	Jumps to the address 400DH if carry flag is 0.
400B	40		
400C	0C	INR C	Increment carry register
400D	05	DCR B	Decrement B register
400E	C2		
400F	08	JNZ **4008H**	Repeat block from 4008H until 'B' is zero
4010	40		
4011	32		
4012	03	STA 5003H	Store the LSB of product in 5003H
4013	50		
4014	79	MOV A, C	Move carry to the accumulator
4015	32		
4016	04	STA 5004H	Store the MSB of product in 5004H
4017	50		
4018	76	HLT	Terminate program execution

Experimental Results:

| Input Data | | Result | |
Memory location	Operand	Memory location	Operand
5000	06 H	5003	18 H (Product-LSB)
5001	04 H	5004	00 H (Product-MSB)

Calculation:

I/O	in HEX
Multiplicand	06 H
Multiplier	04 H
Product	Multiplicand x Multiplier
18H	06H x 04H
Product (LSB)	18 H
Product (MSB)	00 H

Conclusion:

The multiplication of two 8-bit numbers is performed using 8085 microprocessor.

1.10	DIVISION OF TWO 8-BIT NUMBERS

Aim:

Write an 8085 assembly language program to perform the division of two 8-bit binary numbers.

Apparatus:

o   8085 Microprocessor Trainer

Algorithm:

1.   Clear C register for storing the quotient
2.   Initialize the memory location 5000H in H-L register pair for giving input data
3.   Get the dividend in A register
4.   Increment H-L pair to point out the divisor
5.   Move the divisor to B register
6.   Compare dividend and divisor
7.   Check whether the carry flag C is set or not
8.   If C is set, jump to step11
9.   Subtract B reg. from A reg. and increment the quotient register

10. Jump to step 6

11. Store the remainder in the memory location 5003H and quotient in the memory location 5004H

Program:

Memory address	Machine Codes	Mnemonics & Operand(s)	Comments
4000	0E	MVI C, 00H	Clear C register for quotient
4001	00		
4002	21	LXI H, 5000H	Load H-L pair with 5000H to get inputs
4003	00		
4004	50		
4005	7E	MOV A, M	Get the dividend in B register
4006	23	INX H	Increment H-L pair
4007	46	MOV B, M	Get the divisor in A register
4008	B8	CMP B	Compare A reg. and B reg.
4009	DA	JC **4011H**	Jump on carry to the address 4011H.
400A	11		
400B	40		
400C	90	SUB B	Subtract A reg. and B reg.
400D	0C	INR C	Increment C register
400E	C3	JMP **4008H**	Jump to 4008H
400F	08		
4010	40		
4011	32	STA 5003H	Store the remainder in 5003H
4012	03		
4013	50		
4014	79	MOV A, C	Move quotient to the accumulator
4015	32	STA 5004H	Store the quotient in 5004H
4016	04		
4017	50		
4018	76	HLT	Terminate program execution

Experimental Results:

Input Data		Result	
Memory location	Operand	Memory location	Operand
5000	19 H	5003	01 H (remainder)
5001	03 H	5004	08 H (quotient)

Calculation:

I/O	in HEX
Dividend	19 H
Divisor	03 H
Quotient	Dividend / Divisor 19H / 03H
Remainder	01 H
Quotient	08 H

Conclusion:

The division of two 8-bit numbers is performed using 8085 microprocessor.

1.11	1'S COMPLIMENT OF AN 8-BIT NUMBER

Aim:

Write an 8085 assembly language program to perform the 1's compliment of an 8-bit number.

Apparatus:

o 8085 Microprocessor Trainer

Algorithm:

1. Load the 8-bit input data from the memory location 5000H in the accumulator

2. Complement the accumulator

3. Store the accumulator value into memory location 5001H

Program:

Memory address	Machine Codes	Mnemonics & Operand(s)	Comments
4000	3A		
4001	00	LDA 5000H	Load the 8-bit number stored at 5000H in accumulator
4002	50		
4003	2F	CMA	Complement the accumulator.
4004	32		
4005	01	STA 5001H	Store the result in 5001H
4006	50		
4007	76	HLT	Terminate program execution

Experimental Results:

Input Data		Result	
Memory location	Operand	Memory location	Operand
5000	75 H	5001	8A H

Calculation:

I/O	in HEX		in Binary	
Operand	75 H		0111	0101
Result	8A H		1000	1010

Conclusion:

The 1's compliment of an 8-bit number is performed using 8085 microprocessor.

1.12   2'S COMPLIMENT OF AN 8-BIT NUMBER

Aim:

Write an 8085 assembly language program to perform the 2's compliment of an 8-bit number.

Apparatus:

o   8085 Microprocessor Trainer

Algorithm:

1. Load the 8-bit input data from the memory location 5000H in the accumulator
2. Complement the accumulator
3. Add '1' with the complemented value for 2's complement
3. Store the accumulator value into the memory location 5001H

Program:

Memory address	Machine Codes	Mnemonics & Operand(s)	Comments
4000	3A	LDA 5000H	Load the 8-bit number stored at 5000H in accumulator
4001	00		
4002	50		
4003	2F	CMA	Complement the accumulator.
4004	C6	ADI 01H	Add 01H with the accumulator to get 2's complement number.
4005	01		
4006	32	STA 5001H	Store the result in 5001H
4007	01		
4008	50		
4009	76	HLT	Terminate program execution

Experimental Results:

Input Data		Result	
Memory location	Operand	Memory location	Operand
5000	75 H	5001	8B H

Calculation:

I/O	in HEX		in Binary	
Operand	75 H		0111	0101
1's complement			1000	1010
Add 01H			0000	0001
Result	8B H		1000	1011

Conclusion:

The 2's compliment of an 8-bit number is performed using 8085 microprocessor.

1.13 | LARGEST NUMBER IN AN ARRAY

Aim:

Write an 8085 assembly language program to find the largest number from an array of N 8-bit numbers.

Apparatus:

- o 8085 Microprocessor Trainer

Algorithm:

1. Initialize the memory location in H-L register pair for giving input data; H-L points 5000H
2. Move the first data of an array (number of array elements) to C register
3. Clear the accumulator

4. Increment the H-L register pair to point out the next operand
5. Compare the accumulator and the content of memory location pointed by H-L pair
6. Check whether the carry C is generated or not
7. If C is reset, jump to step 9
8. If C is set, move the content of memory to the accumulator (Keep larger value at A reg.)
9. Increment the H-L register pair
10. Decrement the value of C register, which is used as a counter
11. If the counter is non-zero value, repeat the functions from step 5. Otherwise stores the largest number in memory location 5010H

Program:

Memory address	Machine Codes	Mnemonics & Operand(s)	Comments
4000	21		Initialize the memory location 5000H in H-L register pair for input
4001	00	LXI H, 5000H	
4002	50		
4003	4E	MOV C, M	Move the number of array elements to C register
4004	AF	XRA A	Clear the accumulator
4005	23	INX H	Increment H-L pair
4006	BE	CMP M	Compare the content of memory with the accumulator
4007	D2		
4008	0B	JNC **400BH**	If no carry, jump to 400BH
4009	40		
400A	7E	MOV A, M	Move the larger number to the accumulator
400B	23	INX H	Increment H-L pair
400C	0D	DCR C	Decrement C register
400D	C2	JNZ **4006H**	Repeat block from 4006H until

400E	06		'C' is zero
400F	40		
4010	32	STA 5010H	Store the largest number in 5010H
4011	10		
4012	50		
4013	76	HLT	Terminate program execution

Experimental Results:

Input Data		Result	
Memory location	Operand	Memory location	Operand
5000	04 H*	5010	CD H
5001	56 H	-	-
5002	92 H	-	-
5003	13 H	-	-
5004	CD H	-	-

* Number of array elements

Conclusion:

The program to find the largest element in an array of N 8-bit numbers using 8085 microprocessor has been executed.

| 1.14 | SMALLEST NUMBER IN AN ARRAY |

Aim:

Write an 8085 assembly language program to find the smallest number from an array of N 8-bit numbers.

Apparatus:

o   8085 Microprocessor Trainer

Algorithm:

1. Initialize the memory location in H-L register pair for giving input data; H-L points 5000H
2. Move the first data of an array (number of array elements) to C register
3. Clear the accumulator
4. Increment the H-L register pair to point out the next operand
5. Compare the accumulator and the content of memory location pointed by H-L pair
6. Check whether the carry C is generated or not
7. If C is set, jump to step 9
8. If C is reset, move the content of memory to the accumulator (Keep smaller value at A reg.)
9. Increment the H-L register pair
10. Decrement the value of C register, which is used as a counter
11. If the counter is non-zero value, repeat the functions from step 5. Otherwise stores the largest number in memory location 5010H

Program:

Memory address	Machine Codes	Mnemonics & Operand(s)	Comments
4000	21	LXI H, 5000H	Initialize the memory location 5000H in H-L register pair for input
4001	00		
4002	50		
4003	4E	MOV C, M	Move the number of array elements to C register
4004	3E	MVI A, FFH	Move FFH to the accumulator.
4005	FF		
4006	23	INX H	Increment H-L pair
4007	BE	CMP M	Compare the content of memory with the accumulator

4008	D2		If carry flag is set, jump to 400CH
4009	0C	JC **400CH**	
400A	40		
400B	7E	MOV A, M	Move the smaller number to the accumulator
400C	23	INX H	Increment H-L pair
400D	0D	DCR C	Decrement C register
400E	C2		Repeat block from 4007H until 'C' is zero
400F	07	JNZ **4007H**	
4010	40		
4011	32		Store the smallest number in 5010H
4012	10	STA 5010H	
4013	50		
4014	76	HLT	Terminate program execution

Experimental Results:

Input Data		Result	
Memory location	Operand	Memory location	Operand
5000	04 H*	5010	13 H
5001	56 H	-	-
5002	92 H	-	-
5003	13 H	-	-
5004	CD H	-	-

Number of array elements

Conclusion:

The program to find the smallest element in an array of N 8-bit numbers using 8085 microprocessor has been executed.

1.15	DESCENDING ORDER OF AN ARRAY

Aim:

Write an 8085 assembly language program to sort an array of 8-bit binary numbers in descending order.

Apparatus:

o   8085 Microprocessor Trainer

Algorithm:

1.   Initialize the memory location in H-L register pair for giving input data; H-L points 5000H
2.   Move the count value (number of array elements) into B register and Decrement B register
3.   Move the count value (number of array elements) into C register and Decrement C register
4.   Increment the H-L register pair
5.   Move the array element addressed by H-L pair into A register
6.   Increment the H-L register pair
7.   Compare the accumulator and the content of memory location pointed by H-L pair
8.   Check whether the carry C is generated or not
9.   If C is reset, jump to step 12
10. If C is set, exchange the contents between current and previous memory location addressed by H-L pair
11. Increment the H-L register pair
12. Decrement the value of C register
13. If the counter is a non-zero value, repeat the functions from step 5
14. Decrement the value of B register
15. If the counter is a non-zero value, repeat the functions from step 3

Program:

Memory address	Machine Codes	Mnemonics & Operand(s)	Comments
4000	21		Initialize the memory location 5000H in H-L register pair for input
4001	00	LXI H, 5000H	
4002	50		
4003	46	MOV B, M	Move the count value to B register
4004	05	DCR B	Decrement B register
4005	4E	MOV C, M	Move the count value to C register
4006	0D	DCR C	Decrement C register
4007	23	INX H	Increment the H-L pair
4008	7E	MOV A, M	Move the content of memory to the accumulator
4009	23	INX H	Increment the H-L pair
400A	BE	CMP M	Compare the content of memory with the accumulator
400B	D2		
400C	13	JNC 4013H	If no carry, jump to 4013H
400D	40		
400E	56	MOV D, M	Move the content of memory into D register
400F	77	MOV M, A	Move the A reg. value into the memory location pointed by H-L pair
4010	2B	DCX H	Decrement the H-L pair
4011	72	MOV M, D	Move the D reg. value into the memory location pointed by H-L pair
4012	23	INX H	Increment the H-L pair
4013	0D	DCR C	Decrement C register

4014	C2	JNZ **4008H**	Repeat block from 4008H until 'C' is zero
4015	08		
4016	40		
4017	21	LXI H, 5000H	Load H-L pair by 5000H
4018	00		
4019	50		
401A	05	DCR B	Decrement B register
401B	C2	JNZ **4005H**	Repeat block from 4005H until 'B' is zero
401C	05		
401D	40		
401E	76	HLT	Terminate program execution

Experimental Results:

Before Execution		After Execution	
Memory location	Operand	Memory location	Operand
5000	04 H*	5000	04 H*
5001	56 H	5001	CD H
5002	92 H	5002	92 H
5003	13 H	5003	56 H
5004	CD H	5004	13 H

Number of array elements

Conclusion:

The program for sorting numbers of an array in descending order has been executed by 8085 microprocessor.

1.16   ASCENDING ORDER OF AN ARRAY

Aim:

Write an 8085 assembly language program to sort an array of 8-bit binary numbers in ascending order.

Apparatus:

- o   8085 Microprocessor Trainer

Algorithm:

1. Initialize the memory location in H-L register pair for giving input data; H-L points 5000H
2. Move the count value (number of array elements) into B register and Decrement B register
3. Move the count value (number of array elements) into C register and Decrement C register
4. Increment the H-L register pair
5. Move the array element addressed by H-L pair into A register
6. Increment the H-L register pair
7. Compare the accumulator and the content of memory location pointed by H-L pair
8. Check whether the carry C is generated or not
9. If C is set, jump to step 12
10. If C is reset, exchange the contents between current and previous memory location addressed by H-L pair
11. Increment the H-L register pair
12. Decrement the value of C register
13. If the counter is a non-zero value, repeat the functions from step 5
14. Decrement the value of B register
15. If the counter is a non-zero value, repeat the functions from step 3

Program:

Memory address	Machine Codes	Mnemonics & Operand(s)	Comments
4000	21		Initialize the memory location
4001	00	LXI H, 5000H	5000H in H-L register pair for
4002	50		input
4003	46	MOV B, M	Move the count value to B register
4004	05	DCR B	Decrement B register
4005	4E	MOV C, M	Move the count value to C register
4006	0D	DCR C	Decrement C register
4007	23	INX H	Increment the H-L pair
4008	7E	MOV A, M	Move the content of memory to the accumulator
4009	23	INX H	Increment the H-L pair
400A	BE	CMP M	Compare the content of memory with the accumulator
400B	DA		
400C	13	JC 4013H	If carry is set, jump to 4013H
400D	40		
400E	56	MOV D, M	Move the content of memory into D register
400F	77	MOV M, A	Move the A reg. value into the memory location pointed by H-L pair
4010	2B	DCX H	Decrement the H-L pair
4011	72	MOV M, D	Move the D reg. value into the memory location pointed by H-L pair
4012	23	INX H	Increment the H-L pair
4013	0D	DCR C	Decrement C register

4014	C2		
4015	08	JNZ **4008H**	Repeat block from 4008H until 'C' is zero
4016	40		
4017	21		
4018	00	LXI H, 5000H	Load H-L pair by 5000H
4019	50		
401A	05	DCR B	Decrement B register
401B	C2		
401C	05	JNZ **4005H**	Repeat block from 4005H until 'B' is zero
401D	40		
401E	76	HLT	Terminate program execution

Experimental Results:

Before Execution		After Execution	
Memory location	**Operand**	**Memory location**	**Operand**
5000	04 H*	5000	04 H*
5001	56 H	5001	13 H
5002	92 H	5002	56 H
5003	13 H	5003	92 H
5004	CD H	5004	CD H

* Number of array elements

Conclusion:

The program for sorting numbers of an array in ascending order has been executed by 8085 microprocessor.

| 1.17 | BLOCK DATA TRANSFER |

Aim:

Write an 8085 assembly language program to transfer N bytes of data from one memory to another memory block.

Apparatus:

o   8085 Microprocessor Trainer

Algorithm:

1.   Initialize the counter value in C register
2.   Initialize the source memory address 5010H in H-L register pair
3.   Initialize the destination memory address 5020H in D-E register pair
4.   Move the memory content pointed by H-L pair to the accumulator
5.   Store the accumulator to the memory location addressed by D-E pair
6.   Increment the pointer of the source memory block
7.   Increment the pointer of the destination memory block
8.   Decrement the value of C register, which is used as a counter
9.   If the counter is a non-zero value, repeat the functions from step 4. Otherwise stops the program execution

Program:

Memory address	Machine Codes	Mnemonics & Operand(s)	Comments
4000	0E	MVI C, 05H	Initialize the counter value (05H)
4001	05		
4002	21	LXI H, 5010H	Source memory pointer in 5010H
4003	10		
4004	50		
4005	11	LXI D, 5020H	Destination memory pointer in 5020H

4006	20		
4007	50		
4008	7E	MOV A, M	Move the byte from source memory block into the accumulator
4009	12	STAX D	Store the accumulator in the destination memory block
400A	23	INX H	Increment source memory pointer
400B	13	INX D	Increment destination memory pointer
400C	0D	DCR C	Decrement the counter register
400D	C2		
400E	08	JNZ **4008H**	Repeat block from 4008H until 'C' is zero
400F	40		
4010	76	HLT	Terminate program execution

Experimental Results:

Before Execution		After Execution	
Memory location	Operand	Memory location	Operand
5010	54 H	5020	54 H
5011	23 H	5021	23 H
5012	A4 H	5022	A4 H
5013	49 H	5023	49 H
5014	B7 H	5024	B7 H

Conclusion:

Thus the assembly language program for block data transfer has been executed using 8085 microprocessor.

1.18 | FIBONACCI SERIES

Aim:

Write an 8085 assembly language program to find N elements of the Fibonacci series in 8-bit binary.

Apparatus:

o   8085 Microprocessor Trainer

Algorithm:

1. Initialize the memory address 5000H in H-L register pair for giving input
2. Move the counter value to C register
3. Increment the H-L register pair and move 00H to B register
4. Move the content of B register into the memory location pointed by H-L pair
5. Increment the H-L register pair and move 01H to the D register
6. Move the content of D register into the memory location pointed by H-L pair
7. Move the content of B register into A register
8. Add A register and D register
9. Move the content of D register into the B register
10. Move the content of A register into the D register
11. Increment the H-L register pair and decrement counter register
12. If the counter is a non-zero value, repeat the functions from step 6. Otherwise stops the program execution

Program:

Memory address	Machine Codes	Mnemonics & Operand(s)	Comments
4000	21		
4001	00	LXI H, 5000H	Load 5000H in H-L pair
4002	50		

4003	4E	MOV C, M	Move the content of memory pointed by H-L pair to C reg.
4004	23	INX H	Increment the H-L pair
4005	06	MVI B, 00H	Clear B register
4006	00		
4007	70	MOV M, B	Move the content of B reg. to the memory location pointed by H-L pair
4008	23	INX H	Increment the H-L pair
4009	16	MVI D, 01H	Move 01H to D register
400A	01		
400B	72	MOV M, D	Move the content of D reg. to the memory location pointed by H-L pair
400C	78	MOV A, B	Move the content of B reg. into A reg.
400D	82	ADD D	Add accumulator with D register
400E	42	MOV B, D	Move the content of D reg. into B reg.
400F	57	MOV D, A	Move the content of A reg. into D reg.
4010	23	INX H	Increment the H-L pair
4011	0D	DCR C	Increment the C register
4012	C2	JNZ **400BH**	Check the counter has non-zero value; if yes, jump to 400BH
4013	0B		
4014	40		
4015	76	HLT	Terminate program execution

Experimental Results:

Before Execution		After Execution	
Memory location	Operand	Memory location	Operand
5000	0A H	5000	0A H

5001		5001	00 H
5002		5002	01 H
5003		5003	01 H
5004		5004	02 H
5005		5005	03 H
5006		5006	05 H
5007		5007	08 H
5008		5008	0D H
5009		5009	15 H
500A		500A	22 H
500B		500B	37 H

Conclusion:

Thus the assembly language program for Fibonacci series has been executed using 8085 microprocessor.

1.19	BCD TO BINARY CONVERSION

Aim:

Write an 8085 assembly language program to convert a BCD number into a binary number.

Apparatus:

o   8085 Microprocessor Trainer

Algorithm:

1. Load the BCD number from the memory location 5000H into the accumulator
2. Move the accumulator's value to B
3. Obtain BCD-1 by masking the accumulator with 0FH and store it in C register
4. Get the original value in the accumulator by moving B to A
5. Obtain BCD-2 by masking the accumulator with F0H and rotate

this number 4 times right, move it to B register

6. Clear the accumulator
7. Add D to accumulator B number of times
8. Check the carry, if it is not set to repeat from step 7
9. Add C to the accumulator and store the binary result in 5001H
10. Stops the program execution

Program:

Memory address	Machine Codes	Mnemonics & Operand(s)	Comments
4000	3A		
4001	00	LDA 5000H	Get the BCD number
4002	50		
4003	47	MOV B, A	Move the content of A reg. to B reg.
4004	E6	ANI 0FH	Mask most significant four bits
4005	0F		
4006	4F	MOV C, A	Save unpacked BCD-1 in C register
4007	78	MOV A, B	Again get BCD number
4008	E6	ANI 0F0H	Mask least significant four bits
4009	F0		
400A	0F	RRC	
400B	0F	RRC	Convert MSB four bits into unpacked BCD-2
400C	0F	RRC	
400D	0F	RRC	
400E	47	MOV B, A	Save unpacked BCD-2 in B register
400F	AF	XRA A	Clear Accumulator
4010	16	MVI D, 0AH	Move 10 to D reg. for multiplication
4011	0A		

45

4012	82	ADD D	Add 10 until B reg.
4013	05	DCR B	Decrement B reg.
4014	C2		Jump to the location 4012 until non-zero of B reg.
4015	12	JNZ 4012	
4016	40		
4017	81	ADD C	Add C with A
4018	32		Store the binary result in the location 5001H
4019	01	STA 5001H	
401A	50		
401B	76	HLT	Terminate program execution

Experimental Results:

Before Execution		After Execution	
Memory location	Operand	Memory location	Operand
5000	25 H	5000	25 H
5001	-	5001	19 H

Calculation:

Step	BCD	Binary Number
1	25	2 | 25 2 | 12 --- 1 2 | 6 --- 0 2 | 3 --- 0 1 --- 1
2	-	0001 1001
3	-	19 H

Conclusion:

Thus the assembly language program for BCD to binary conversion has been executed using 8085 microprocessor.

| 1.20 | BINARY TO BCD CONVERSION |

Aim:

Write an 8085 assembly language program to convert a binary number into its equivalent BCD number.

Apparatus:

- 8085 Microprocessor Trainer

Algorithm:

1. Set memory pointer at 5000H for getting binary input value
2. Clear D register and A register
3. Move the input value to C register
4. Add 01H with accumulator and adjust it to the decimal
5. Check the carry, if it is not set jump to step 7
6. Increment D register
7. Decrement C register
8. Jump to step 4 until setting zero flag
9. Move the MSB and LSB of BCD number to H-L pair
10. Store the BCD result at 5001H and 5002H
11. Stops the program execution

Program:

Memory address	Machine Codes	Mnemonics & Operand(s)	Comments
4000	21		Initialize memory pointer at 5000H for receiving input
4001	00	LXI H, 5000H	
4002	50		
4003	16	MVI D,00H	Clear D register
4004	00		
4005	AF	XRA A	Clear Accumulator
4006	4E	MOV C, M	Get binary/Hex data in C

			register
4007	C6	ADI 01H	Count the number one by one
4008	01		
4009	27	DAA	Decimal adjust for BCD count
400A	D2	JNC **400EH**	Jump on no carry to 400E
400B	0E		
400C	40		
400D	14	INR D	Increment D register
400E	0D	DCR C	Decrement C register
400F	C2	JNZ **4007H**	Jump on no zero to 4007
4010	07		
4011	40		
4012	6F	MOV L, A	Load the LSB in L register
4013	62	MOV H, D	Load the MSB in H register
4014	22	SHLD 5001H	Store the BCD number in 5001H and 5002H
4015	01		
4016	50		
4017	76	HLT	Terminate program execution

Experimental Results:

Before Execution		After Execution	
Memory location	Operand	Memory location	Operand
5000	19 H	5000	19 H
5001	-	5001	25 H

Calculation:

Step	Binary Number	Decimal Number
1	0001 1001	$((1 \times 2^4) + (1 \times 2^3) + (0 \times 2^2) + (0 \times 2^1) + (1 \times 2^0))$

2		16 + 8 + 0+ 0 + 1
3		25

Conclusion:

Thus the assembly language program for binary to BCD conversion has been executed using 8085 microprocessor.

1.21	BINARY TO ASCII CONVERSION

Aim:

Write an 8085 assembly language program to convert a binary number into its equivalent ASCII number.

Apparatus:

- o 8085 Microprocessor Trainer

Algorithm:

1. Set memory pointer at 5000H for getting binary input value
2. Move the input data to the accumulator
3. Move the accumulator to the B register
4. Clear carry flag
4. Substrate 0AH from the accumulator
5. Jump to step 8 if carry is set
6. Add 41H to the accumulator
7. Jump to step 10
8. Move B register to the accumulator
9. Add 30H to the accumulator
10. Increment the H-L register pair
11. Move accumulator to the memory location which is pointed by H-L pair
12. Terminate the program

Program:

Memory address	Machine Codes	Mnemonics & Operand(s)	Comments
4000	21		
4001	00	LXI H, 5000H	Initialize memory pointer at 5000H for receiving input
4002	50		
4003	7E	MOV A, M	Move the input data to the accumulator
4004	47	MOV B, A	Move accumulator to B reg.
4005	37	STC	Set the Carry flag
4006	3F	CMC	Complement Carry
4007	D6	SUI 0AH	Substrate 0AH from accumulator
4008	0A		
4009	DA		
400A	0E	JC **4011H**	Jump on carry to 400E
400B	40		
400C	C6	ADI 41H	Add 41H with the accumulator
400D	41		
400E	C3		
400F	14	JMP **4014H**	Jump to 4007
4010	40		
4011	78	MOV A, B	Move B reg. to A reg.
4012	C6	ADI 30H	Add 30H with the accumulator
4013	30		
4014	23	INX H	Increment H-L pair
4015	77	MOV M, A	Move accumulator to memory location pointed by H-L pair
4016	76	HLT	Terminate program execution

Experimental Results:

Before Execution		After Execution	
Memory location	Operand	Memory location	Operand
5000	05 H	5000	05 H
5001	-	5001	35 H

Before Execution		After Execution	
Memory location	Operand	Memory location	Operand
5000	0E H	5000	0E H
5001	-	5001	45 H

Calculation:

Step	Binary Number	ASCII Number
1	05 H	05 – 0A (Carry will set) 05 + 30 = 35 H
2	0E H	0E – 0A = 04 H (No carry) 04 + 41 = 45 H

Conclusion:

Thus the assembly language program for binary to ASCII conversion has been executed using 8085 microprocessor.

| 1.22 | ASCII TO BINARY CONVERSION |

Aim:

Write an 8085 assembly language program to convert an ASCII number into its equivalent binary number.

Apparatus:

o   8085 Microprocessor Trainer

Algorithm:

1. Set memory pointer at 5000H for getting ASCII input value
2. Move the input data to the accumulator
3. Subtract 30H from the accumulator
4. Compare the content of accumulator with 0AH
5. If the value of accumulator is less than 0AH then jump to step 7
6. Subtract 07H from the accumulator
7. Increment the H-L register pair
8. Move accumulator to the memory location which is pointed by H-L pair
9. Terminate the program execution

Program:

Memory address	Machine Codes	Mnemonics & Operand(s)	Comments
4000	21		Initialize memory pointer at 5000H for receiving input
4001	00	LXI H, 5000H	
4002	50		
4003	7E	MOV A, M	Move the input data to the accumulator
4004	D6	SUI 30H	Subtract 30H from the accumulator
4005	30		
4006	FE	CPI 0AH	Compare accumulator with 0AH
4007	0A		
4008	DA		
4009	0D	JC 400DH	Jump to 400DH if carry is set
400A	40		
400B	D6	SUI 07H	Substrate 07H from the accumulator
400C	07		
400D	23	INX H	Increment H-L pair
400E	77	MOV M, A	Move accumulator to memory location pointed by H-L pair
400F	76	HLT	Terminate program execution

Experimental Results:

Before Execution		After Execution	
Memory location	Operand	Memory location	Operand
5000	37 H	5000	37 H
5001	-	5001	07 H

Before Execution		After Execution	
Memory location	Operand	Memory location	Operand
5000	44 H	5000	44 H
5001	-	5001	0D H

Calculation:

Step	Binary Number	ASCII Number
1	37 H	37H – 30H = 07H 07H – 0AH (Carry will set) = 07H is ASCII number
2	44 H	44H – 30H = 14 H 14H – 0AH (No carry) 14H – 07H = 0D H

Conclusion:

Thus the assembly language program for ASCII to binary conversion has been executed using 8085 microprocessor.

1.23	BINARY TO GRAY CONVERSION

Aim:

Write an 8085 microprocessor assembly language program to convert Binary code into Gray code.

Apparatus:

o   8085 Microprocessor Trainer

Algorithm:

1. Set memory pointer at 5000H for getting binary input value
2. Move the input data to the accumulator
3. Move the accumulator value to the D register
4. Rotate Accumulator right
5. XOR the accumulator with D register
6. Increment the H-L register pair
7. Move accumulator to the memory location which is pointed by H-L pair
8. Terminate the program execution

Program:

Memory address	Machine Codes	Mnemonics & Operand(s)	Comments
4000	21		
4001	00	LXI H, 5000H	Initialize memory pointer at 5000H for receiving input
4002	50		
4003	7E	MOV A, M	Move the input data to the accumulator
4004	57	MOV D, A	Move accumulator content in to D register accumulator
4005	1F	RAR	Rotate accumulator right
4006	AA	XRA D	Exclusive OR the content of D register
4007	23	INX H	Increment H-L pair
4008	77	MOV M, A	Move accumulator to memory location pointed by H-L pair
4009	76	HLT	Terminate program execution

Calculation:

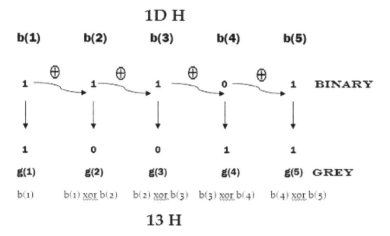

1D H

b(1) b(2) b(3) b(4) b(5)

1 ⊕ 1 ⊕ 1 ⊕ 0 ⊕ 1   BINARY

1 0 0 1 1

g(1) g(2) g(3) g(4) g(5) GREY

b(1) b(1) xor b(2) b(2) xor b(3) b(3) xor b(4) b(4) xor b(5)

13 H

Experimental Results:

Before Execution		After Execution	
Memory location	Operand	Memory location	Operand
5000	1D H	5000	1D H
5001	-	5001	13 H

Conclusion:

Thus the assembly language program for binary to gray code conversion has been executed using 8085 microprocessor.

1.24   **GRAY TO BINARY CONVERSION**

Aim:

Write an 8085 microprocessor assembly language program to convert Grey code into Binary code.

Apparatus:

- o   8085 Microprocessor Trainer

Algorithm:

1. Set memory pointer at 5000H for getting Gray code input value
2. Move the input data to the accumulator
3. Move the accumulator value to the D register
4. Move the data 07H to the C register
5. Set carry and Complement carry
6. Rotate Accumulator right
7. XOR the accumulator with D register
8. Decrement C register
9. Jump to step 5 if C register is non zero
10. Increment the H-L register pair
11. Move accumulator to the memory location which is pointed by H-L pair
12. Terminate the program execution

Program:

Memory address	Machine Codes	Mnemonics & Operand(s)	Comments
4000	21	LXI H, 5000H	Initialize memory pointer at 5000H for receiving input
4001	00		
4002	50		
4003	7E	MOV A, M	Move the content pointed by H-L pair to accumulator
4004	57	MOV D, A	Move accumulator content in to D register accumulator
4005	0E	MVI C, 07H	Move the data 07 in C
4006	07		
4007	37	STC	Set carry
4008	3F	CMC	Complement carry
4009	1F	RAR	Rotate accumulator right
400A	AA	XRA D	Exclusive OR the content of D register

400B	0D	DCR C	Increment H-L pair
400C	C2	JNZ **4007H**	Jump to 4007H if C register having non zero value
400D	06		
400E	40		
400F	23	INX H	Increment H-L pair
4010	77	MOV M, A	Move accumulator to memory location pointed by H-L pair
4011	76	HLT	Terminate program execution

Experimental Results:

Before Execution		After Execution	
Memory location	Operand	Memory location	Operand
5000	13 H	5000	13 H
5001	-	5001	1D H

Calculation:

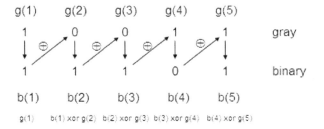

Conclusion:

Thus the assembly language program for gray code to binary code conversion has been executed using 8085 microprocessor.

1.25	SAWTOOTH WAVEFORM GENERATION USING 8255

Aim:

Write a program to generate continuous sawtooth waveform using 8085uP and 8255 PPI.

Apparatus:

- o   8085 Microprocessor Trainer
- o   8255 PPI and DAC 0808 module

Algorithm:

1.   Move 80H to the control word register of 8255 for all ports output
2.   Move the initial value 00H to the accumulator
3.   Move the accumulator value to the Port A of 8255
4.   Increment Accumulator
5.   Compare the content of accumulator with FFH
6.   Jump to step 3 until the zero flag is set
7.   Jump to step 2

Program:

Memory address	Machine Codes	Mnemonics & Operand(s)	Comments
4000	3E	MVI A, 80H	Move 80H to A register
4001	80		
4002	D3	OUT 83H	Send the content of A register to control word register of 8255
4003	83		
4004	3E	MVI A, 00H	Move 00H to A register
4005	00		
4006	D3	OUT 80H	Send the content of A register to Port A of 8255

4007	80		
4008	3C	INR A	Increment Accumulator
4009	D3	OUT 80H	Send the content of A register to Port A of 8255
400A	80		
400B	FE	CPI FFH	Compare the content of A register with FFH
400C	FF		
400D	C2	JNZ **4008H**	Jump to 4008H until the zero flag is set
400E	08		
400F	40		
4010	C3	JMP **4004H**	Jump to 4004H
4011	04		
4012	40		

Control Word of 8255:

Table

D7	D6	D5	D4	D3	D2	D1	D0	Control Word	PORT A	PORT C Upper	PORT B	PORT C Lower
1	0	0	0	0	0	0	0	80 H	Output	Output	Output	Output
1	0	0	0	0	0	0	1	81 H	Output	Output	Output	Input
1	0	0	0	0	0	1	0	82 H	Output	Output	Input	Output
1	0	0	0	0	0	1	1	83 H	Output	Output	Input	Input
1	0	0	0	1	0	0	0	88 H	Output	Input	Output	Output
1	0	0	0	1	0	0	1	89 H	Output	Input	Output	Input
1	0	0	0	1	0	1	0	8A H	Output	Input	Input	Output
1	0	0	0	1	0	1	1	8B H	Output	Input	Input	Input
1	0	0	1	0	0	0	0	90 H	Input	Output	Output	Output
1	0	0	1	0	0	0	1	91 H	Input	Output	Output	Input
1	0	0	1	0	0	1	0	92 H	Input	Output	Input	Output
1	0	0	1	0	0	1	1	93 H	Input	Output	Input	Input
1	0	0	1	1	0	0	0	98 H	Input	Input	Output	Output
1	0	0	1	1	0	0	1	99 H	Input	Input	Output	Input
1	0	0	1	1	0	1	0	9A H	Input	Input	Input	Output
1	0	0	1	1	0	1	1	9B H	Input	Input	Input	Input

Experimental Results:

Circuit Diagram:

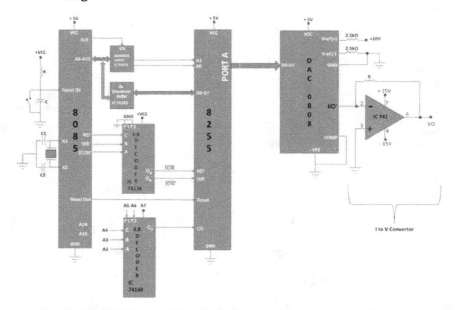

The DAC 0808 is an 8-bit digital to analog converter. It converts a digital value into the equivalent analog current. Hence I to V converter is used to convert analog output current to an equivalent analog voltage. The Port A (PA0-PA7) pins are connected to D0-D7 pins of DAC 0808. Connect the CRO/DSO probe in the output of I to V converter.

Conclusion:

Thus the assembly language program for generating sawtooth waveform has been executed using 8085 microprocessor.

1.26	TRIANGULAR WAVEFORM GENERATION USING 8255

Aim:

Write a program to generate continuous triangular waveform using 8085uP and 8255 PPI.

Apparatus:

- o 8085 Microprocessor Trainer
- o 8255 PPI and DAC 0808 module

Algorithm:

1. Move 80H to the control word register of 8255 for all ports output
2. Move the initial value 00H to the accumulator
3. Move the accumulator value to the Port A of 8255
4. Increment Accumulator
5. Compare the content of accumulator with FFH
6. Jump to step 3 until the zero flag is set
7. Decrement Accumulator
8. Send the content of accumulator to Port A of 8255
9. Compare the content of accumulator with 00H
10. Jump to step 7 until the zero flag is set
11. Jump to step 2

Program:

Memory address	Machine Codes	Mnemonics & Operand(s)	Comments
4000	3E	MVI A, 80H	Move 80H to A register
4001	80		
4002	D3	OUT 83H	Send the content of A register to control word register of 8255
4003	83		

4004	3E	MVI A, 00H	Move 00H to A register
4005	00		
4006	D3	OUT 80H	Send the content of A register to Port A of 8255
4007	80		
4008	3C	INR A	Increment Accumulator
4009	D3	OUT 80H	Send the content of A register to Port A of 8255
400A	80		
400B	FE	CPI FFH	Compare the content of A register with FFH
400C	FF		
400D	C2	JNZ **4008H**	Jump to 4008H until the zero flag is set
400E	08		
400F	40		
4010	3D	DCR A	Decrement Accumulator
4011	D3	OUT 80H	Send the content of A register to Port A of 8255
4012	80		
4013	FE	CPI 00H	Compare the content of A register with 00H
4014	00		
4015	C2	JNZ **4010H**	Jump to 4010H until the zero flag is set
4016	10		
4017	40		
4018	C3	JMP **4004H**	Jump to 4004H
4019	04		
401A	40		

Circuit Diagram:

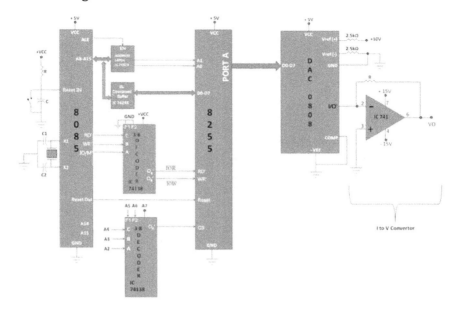

Experimental Results:

The DAC 0808 is an 8-bit digital to analog converter. It converts a digital value into the equivalent analog current. Hence I to V converter is used to convert analog output current to an equivalent analog voltage. The Port A (PA0-PA7) pins are connected to D0-D7 pins of DAC 0808. Connect the CRO/DSO probe in the output of I to V converter.

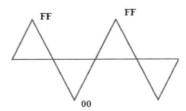

Conclusion:

Thus the assembly language program for generating continuous triangular waveform has been executed using 8085 microprocessor and 8255 PPI.

| 1.27 | SQUARE WAVEFORM GENERATION USING 8255 |

Aim:

Write a program to generate continuous square waveform using 8085uP and 8255 PPI.

Apparatus:

- o 8085 Microprocessor Trainer
- o 8255 PPI and DAC 0808 module

Algorithm:

Main Program:

1. Move 80H to the control word register of 8255 for all ports output
2. Move the initial value 00H to the accumulator
3. Move the accumulator value to the Port A of 8255
4. Call Delay subroutine
5. Move the initial value FFH to the accumulator
6. Move the accumulator value to the Port A of 8255
7. Call Delay subroutine
8. Jump to step 2

Subroutine:

1. Move the count value for delay loop to the B register (AAH).
2. Decrement B register
3. Jump to step 2 until the B register value to zero
4. Return to the main program.

Program:

Memory address	Machine Codes	Mnemonics & Operand(s)	Comments
4000	3E	MVI A, 80H	Move 80H to A register
4001	80		

4002	D3	OUT 83H	Send the content of A register to control word register of 8255
4003	83		
4004	3E	MVI A, 00H	Move 00H to A register
4005	00		
4006	D3	OUT 80H	Send the content of A register to Port A of 8255
4007	80		
4008	CD	CALL **DELAY**	Call Delay subroutine
4009	50		
400A	40		
400B	3E	MVI A, FFH	Move FFH to A register
400C	FF		
400D	D3	OUT 80H	Send the content of A register to Port A of 8255
400E	80		
400F	CD	CALL **DELAY**	Call Delay subroutine
4010	50		
4011	40		
4012	C3	JMP **4004H**	Jump to 4004H
4013	04		
4014	40		
DELAY:			
4050	06	MVI B, AAH	Move the count value AAH to B register for delay
4051	AA		
4052	05	DCR B	Decrement B register
4053	C2	JNZ 4051H	Jump to 4051H until non-zero value of B register
4054	51		
4055	40		
4056	C9	RET	Return to main program

Circuit Diagram:

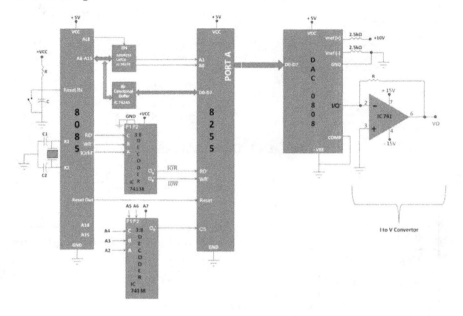

Experimental Results:

The DAC 0808 is an 8-bit digital to analog converter. It converts a digital value into the equivalent analog current. Hence I to V converter is used to convert analog output current to an equivalent analog voltage. The Port A (PA0-PA7) pins are connected to D0-D7 pins of DAC 0808. Connect the CRO/DSO probe in the output of I to V converter.

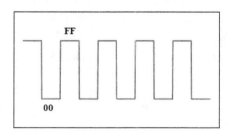

Conclusion:

Thus the assembly language program for generating continuous square waveform has been executed using 8085 microprocessor and 8255 PPI.

| 1.28 | DECADE COUNTER USING 8255 |

Aim:

Write an assembly language program for decade counter using 8085uP and 8255 PPI.

Apparatus:

- o 8085 Microprocessor Trainer
- o 8255 PPI and LEDs

Algorithm:

1. Move 80H to the control word register of 8255 for all ports output
2. Move the initial value 00H to the accumulator
3. Move the accumulator value to the Port A of 8255
4. Call Delay subroutine
5. Increment Accumulator
6. Compare the content of accumulator with *0AH*
7. Jump to step 3 until the zero flag is set
8. Jump to step 2

Program:

Memory address	Machine Codes	Mnemonics & Operand(s)	Comments
4000	3E	MVI A, 80H	Move 80H to A register
4001	80		
4002	D3	OUT 83H	Send the content of A register to control word register of 8255
4003	83		
4004	3E	MVI A, 00H	Move 00H to A register
4005	00		
4006	D3	OUT 80H	Send the content of A register to Port A of 8255
4007	80		
4008	CD	CALL Delay	Call Delay subroutine

4009	50		
400A	40		
400B	3C	INR A	Increment Accumulator
400C	FE	CPI 0AH	Compare the content of A register with 0AH
400D	0A		
400E	C2	JNZ **4006H**	Jump to 4006H until the zero flag is set
400F	06		
4010	40		
4011	C3	JMP **4004H**	Jump to 4004H
4012	04		
4013	40		
Delay:			
4050	06	MVI B, 03H	Move the count value 03H to B register
4051	03		
4052	0E	MVI C, AAH	Move the count value AAH to C register
4053	AA		
4054	16	MVI D, AAH	Move the count value AAH to D register
4055	AA		
4056	15	DCR D	Decrement D register
4057	C2	JNZ **4056H**	Jump to 4056H until non-zero value of D register
4058	56		
4059	40		
405A	0D	DCR C	Decrement C register
405B	C2	JNZ **4054H**	Jump to 4054H until non-zero value of C register
405C	54		
405D	40		
405E	05	DCR B	Decrement B register
405F	C2	JNZ **4052H**	Jump to 4052H until non-zero value of B register
4060	52		
4061	40		
4062	C9	RET	Return to main program

Circuit Diagram:

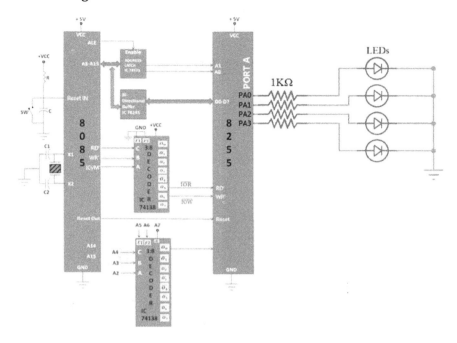

Experimental Results:

PA3	PA2	PA1	PA0
0	0	0	0
0	0	0	1
0	0	1	0
0	0	1	1
0	1	0	0
0	1	0	1
0	1	1	0
0	1	1	1
1	0	0	0
1	0	0	1

Conclusion:

Thus the assembly language program for decade counter has been executed using 8085 microprocessor.

| 1.29 | STEPPER MOTOR CONTROLLER USING 8255 |

Aim:

Write an assembly language program for stepper motor controller using 8085uP and 8255 PPI.

Apparatus:

- o 8085 Microprocessor Trainer
- o 8255 PPI and Stepper motor module

Theory:

A stepper motor is a brushless, synchronous electric motor that converts digital pulses into mechanical shaft rotation. Every revolution of the stepper motor is divided into a discrete number of steps, and the motor must be sent a separate pulse for each step.

The stepper motor is connected with Port-A of 8085 Microprocessor pins through a ULN2803A. The Microprocessor is giving pulses with particular frequency to ULN2803A, the motor is rotated in clockwise or anticlockwise based on the step sequence.

Algorithm:

An algorithm for one complete clockwise rotation of stepper motor as follows,

1. Move 80H to the control word register of 8255 for all ports output
2. Initialize the memory pointer using H-L pair at 5000H
3. Initialize the number of steps in a step sequence in E reg.
4. Move the memory location value to the accumulator
5. Move the accumulator value to the Port A of 8255
6. Call Delay subroutine
7. Increment H-L pair
8. Decrement the step sequence counter (E Reg.)
9. Jump to step 4 until the zero flag is set (E =0)
10. Halt the program execution

Program:

Memory address	Machine Codes	Mnemonics & Operand(s)	Comments
4000	3E	MVI A, 80H	Move 80H to A register
4001	80		
4002	D3	OUT 83H	Send the content of A register to control word register of 8255
4003	83		
4004	21	LXI H, 5000H	Initialize memory pointer at 5000H
4005	00		
4006	50		
4007	1E	MVI E, 04H	Move the number step (04) in a sequence to E register
4008	04		
4009	7E	MOV A, M	Move the content of memory location pointed by H-L pair to the accumulator
400A	D3	OUT 80H	Send the content of A register to Port A of 8255
400B	80		
400C	CD	CALL Delay	Call Delay subroutine
400D	50		
400E	40		
400F	23	INX H	Increment H-L pair
4010	1D	DCR E	Decrement E register
4011	C2	JNZ **4009H**	Jump to 4009H until the zero flag is set
4012	09		
4013	40		
4014	76	HLT	Halt the main program
Delay:			
4050	0E	MVI C, FFH	Move the count value FFH to C register
4051	FF		
4052	16	MVI D, FFH	Move the count value FFH to D

4053	FF		
4054	15	DCR D	Decrement D register
4055	C2	JNZ **4054H**	Jump to 4054H until non-zero value of D register
4056	54		
4057	40		
4058	0D	DCR C	Decrement C register
405A	C2	JNZ **4052H**	Jump to 4052H until non-zero value of C register
405B	52		
405C	40		
405D	C9	RET	Return to main program

Experimental:

Circuit Diagram:

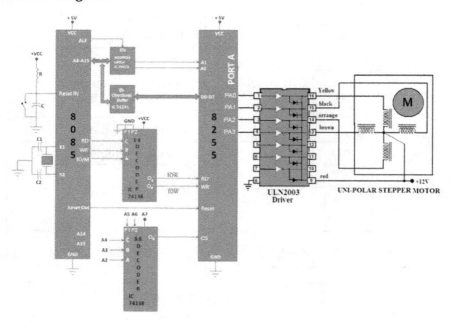

The full step sequence for clockwise rotation is,

Address	PA3	PA2	PA1	PA0	Hex Value
5000	0	0	1	1	03
5001	0	1	1	0	06
5002	1	1	0	0	0C
5003	1	0	0	1	09

The full step sequence for anticlockwise rotation is,

Address	PA3	PA2	PA1	PA0	Hex Value
5000	1	0	0	1	09
5001	1	1	0	0	0C
5002	0	1	1	0	06
5003	0	0	1	1	03

Conclusion:

Thus the assembly language program for stepper motor controller using 8085uP and 8255 PPI has been executed.

| 1.30 | **TRAFFIC LIGHT CONTROLLER USING 8255** |

Aim:

Write an assembly language program for traffic light controller using 8085uP and 8255 PPI.

Apparatus:

- o   8085 Microprocessor Trainer
- o   8255 PPI and Traffic light module

Algorithm:

The below figure shows the traffic lights arrangement of the traffic light system.

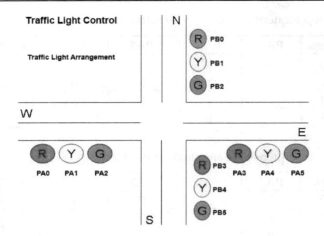

The traffic light sequence for the traffic light controller is described as follows,

1) Allow traffic from W to E and E to W transition for 20 seconds.

2) Give transition time of 4 seconds (Yellow bulbs ON)

3) Allow traffic from N to Sand S to N for 20 seconds

4) Give transition time of 4 seconds (Yellow bulbs ON)

5) Repeat the process.

South			North			East			West			HEX PB/PA
Green	Yellow	Red	Green	Yellow	Red	Green	Yellow	Red	Green	Yellow	Red	
PB5	PB4	PB3	PB2	PB1	PB0	PA5	PA4	PA3	PA2	PA1	PA0	
0	0	1	0	0	1	1	0	0	1	0	0	09/24
Delay for 20 seconds												
0	1	0	0	1	0	0	1	0	0	1	0	12/12
Delay for 4 seconds												
1	0	0	1	0	0	0	0	1	0	0	1	24/09
Delay for 20 seconds												
0	1	0	0	1	0	0	1	0	0	1	0	12/12
Delay for 4 seconds												

1. Move 80H to the control word register of 8255 for all ports output
2. Initialize the memory pointer using H-L pair at 5000H
3. Initialize the number of steps in a traffic sequence in E reg.
4. Move the memory value to the accumulator
5. Move the accumulator value to the Port A of 8255
6. Increment H-L pair
7. Move the accumulator value to the Port B of 8255
8. Call Delay subroutine (20 sec)
9. Increment H-L pair
10. Decrement E register
11. Move the accumulator value to the Port A of 8255
12. Increment H-L pair
13. Move the accumulator value to the Port B of 8255
14. Call Delay subroutine (4 sec)
15. Increment H-L pair
16. Decrement E register
17. Jump to step 4 until the zero flag is set (E =0)
18. Repeat the algorithm from step 2

Program:

Memory address	Machine Codes	Mnemonics & Operand(s)	Comments
4000	3E	MVI A, 80H	Move 80H to A register
4001	80		
4002	D3	OUT 83H	Send the content of A register to control word register of 8255
4003	83		
4004	21	LXI H, 5000H	Initialize memory pointer at 5000H
4005	00		
4006	50		
4007	1E	MVI E, 04H	Move the number step (04) in a sequence to E register
4008	04		

4009	7E	MOV A, M	Move the content of memory location pointed by H-L pair to the accumulator
400A	D3	OUT 80H	Send the content of A register to Port A of 8255
400B	80		
400C	23	INX H	Increment H-L pair
400D	7E	MOV A, M	Move the content of memory location pointed by H-L pair to the accumulator
400E	D3	OUT 81H	Send the content of A register to Port B of 8255
400F	81		
4010	CD	CALL Delay_20	Call Delay subroutine (20 sec)
4011	50		
4012	40		
4013	23	INX H	Increment H-L pair
4014	1D	DCR E	Decrement E register
4015	7E	MOV A, M	Move the content of memory location pointed by H-L pair to the accumulator
4016	D3	OUT 80H	Send the content of A register to Port A of 8255
4017	80		
4018	23	INX H	Increment H-L pair
4019	7E	MOV A, M	Move the content of memory location pointed by H-L pair to the accumulator
401A	D3	OUT 81H	Send the content of A register to Port B of 8255
401B	81		
401C	CD	CALL Delay_4	Call Delay subroutine (4 sec)
401D	70		
401E	40		
401F	23	INX H	Increment H-L pair
4020	1D	DCR E	Decrement E register

4021	C2	JNZ **4009H**	Jump to 4009H until the zero flag is set
4022	09		
4023	40		
4024	C3	JMP **4004H**	Do again
4025	04		
4026	40		

Delay_20: (20 Seconds)

4050	06	MVI B, "<u>20Sec</u>"	Move the count value for 20sec to B register
4051	---		
4052	0E	MVI C, FFH	Move the count value FFH to C register
4053	FF		
4054	16	MVI D, FFH	Move the count value FFH to D register
4055	FF		
4056	15	DCR D	Decrement D register
4057	C2	JNZ **4056H**	Jump to 4056H until non-zero value of D register
4058	56		
405A	40		
405B	0D	DCR C	Decrement C register
405C	C2	JNZ **4054H**	Jump to 4054H until non-zero value of C register
405D	54		
405E	40		
405F	05	DCR B	Decrement B register
4060	C2	JNZ **4052H**	Jump to 4052H until non-zero value of B register
4061	52		
4062	40		
4063	C9	RET	Return to main program

Delay_4: (4 Seconds)

4070	06	MVI B, "<u>4Sec</u>"	Move the count value for 4sec to B register
4071	---		

77

4072	0E	MVI C, FFH	Move the count value FFH to C register
4073	FF		
4074	16	MVI D, FFH	Move the count value FFH to D register
4075	FF		
4076	15	DCR D	Decrement D register
4077	C2	JNZ 4076H	Jump to 4076H until non-zero value of D register
4078	76		
407A	40		
407B	0D	DCR C	Decrement C register
407C	C2	JNZ 4074H	Jump to 4074H until non-zero value of C register
407D	74		
407E	40		
407F	05	DCR B	Decrement B register
4080	C2	JNZ 4072H	Jump to 4072H until non-zero value of B register
4081	72		
4082	40		
4083	C9	RET	Return to main program

Experimental - Inputs:

Address	PB	PA	HEX
5000	-	24	24
5001	09	-	09
5002	-	12	12
5003	12	-	12
5004	-	09	09
5005	24	-	24
5006	-	12	12
5007	12	-	12

Circuit Diagram:

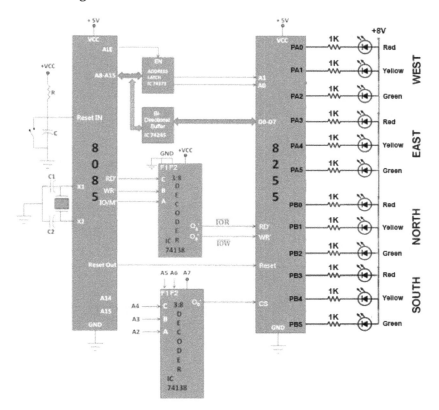

Conclusion:

Thus the assembly language program for traffic light controller using 8085uP and 8255 PPI has been executed.

1.31 | SEVEN SEGMENT DISPLAY INTERFACING

Aim:

Write an assembly language program to interface an 8-digit 7 segment LED display using 8255 to the 8085 microprocessor and write the message on the display.

Apparatus:

- o 8085 Microprocessor Trainer
- o 8255 PPI and Seven segment display module

Algorithm:

In this circuit Port A and Port B are used as output ports. Port A provides the segment data inputs to the display and port B provides a selection input to the display.

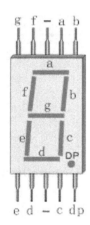

	dp	g	f	e	d	c	b	a	hex value
0	0	0	1	1	1	1	1	1	3F
1	0	0	0	0	0	1	1	0	06
2	0	1	0	1	1	0	1	1	5B
3	0	1	0	0	1	1	1	1	4F
4	0	1	1	0	0	1	1	0	66
5	0	1	1	0	1	1	0	1	6D
6	0	1	1	1	1	1	0	1	7D
7	0	0	0	0	0	1	1	1	07
8	0	1	1	1	1	1	1	1	7F
9	0	1	1	0	1	1	1	1	6F
A	0	1	1	1	0	1	1	1	77
b	0	1	1	1	1	1	0	0	7C
C	0	0	1	1	1	0	0	1	39
d	0	1	0	1	1	1	1	0	5E
E	0	1	1	1	1	0	0	1	79
F	0	1	1	1	0	0	0	1	71

1. Move 80H to the control word register of 8255 for all ports output

2. Initialize the starting address of the message using H-L pair at 5000H

3. Initialize the number of characters to be displayed on screen in C reg.

4. Move 7F to the B register (segment select pattern)
5. Move B reg. value to accumulator
6. Move the accumulator value to the Port B of 8255
7. Rotate right accumulator (RRC)
8. Move accumulator to B register
9. Move the content of memory to accumulator
10. Move the accumulator value to the Port A of 8255
11. Increment H-L pair
12. Decrement C register
13. Jump to step 5 until the zero flag is set (C =0)
14. Repeat the algorithm from step 2

Program:

Memory address	Machine Codes	Mnemonics & Operand(s)	Comments
4000	3E	MVI A, 80H	Move 80H to A register
4001	80		
4002	D3	OUT 83H	Send the content of A register to control word register of 8255
4003	83		
4004	21	LXI H, 5000H	Initialize memory pointer at 5000H
4005	00		
4006	50		
4007	0E	MVI C, 08H	Move the number step (04) in a sequence to E register
4008	08		
4009	06	MVI B, 7FH	Move 7F to the B register (segment select pattern)
400A	7F		
400B	78	MOV A, B	Move B reg to accumulator
400C	D3	OUT 81H	Send the content of A register to Port B of 8255
400D	81		
400E	0F	RRC	Rotate accumulator right
400F	47	MOV B, A	Move accumulator to B reg.
4010	7E	MOV A, M	Move the content of memory location to the accumulator
4011	D3	OUT 80H	Send the content of A register to Port A of 8255
4012	80		

4013	23	INX H	Increment H-L pair
4014	0D	DCR C	Decrement C register
4015	C2	JNZ **400BH**	Jump to 400BH until the zero flag is set
4016	0B		
4017	40		
4018	C3	JMP **4004H**	Jump to 4004H
4019	04		
401A	40		

Circuit Diagram:

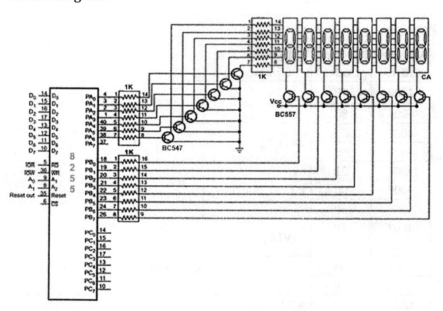

Experimental:

Message	ABCD-123
Address	**HEX (PA)**
5000	77
5001	7C
5002	39
5003	5E

5004	40
5005	06
5006	5B
5007	4F

Conclusion:

Thus the assembly language program for seven segment display interface using 8085uP and 8255 PPI has been executed.

1.32	REAL TIME CLOCK

Aim:

Write an assembly language program to simulate real-time clock using the 8085 microprocessor.

Apparatus:

   o   8085 Microprocessor Trainer

Algorithm:

1. Clear H-L pair for storing Hours and Minutes
2. Clear accumulator
3. Store the content of H-L pair in 5000H
4. Store the accumulator in 5002H
5. Generate delay of 1 second
6. Increment accumulator and adjust to decimal
7. If accumulator < 60, jump to step 3
8. Clear accumulator
9. Increment L reg and adjust to decimal
10. If L reg. < 60, jump to step 3
11. Clear accumulator
12. Increment accumulator and adjust to decimal
13. If H reg. < 60, jump to step 3
14. Clear accumulator
15. Jump to step 3

Program:

Memory address	Machine Codes	Mnemonics & Operand(s)	Comments
4000	21	LXI H, 0000H	Clear H-L pair
4001	00		
4002	00		
4003	AF	XRA A	Clear A register
4004	22	SHLD 5000H	Store L and H in 5000H and 5001H respectively
4005	00		
4006	50		
4007	32	STA 5002H	Store accumulator in 5002H
4008	02		
4009	50		
400A	CD	CALL Delay1s	Call 1sec delay subroutine
400B	50		
400C	40		
400D	3C	INR A	Increment A register
400E	27	DAA	Decimal adjust accumulator
400F	FE	CPI 60H	Compare accumulator with 60H
4010	60		
4011	C2	JNZ 4004H	Jump to 4004H until the zero flag is set
4012	04		
4013	40		
4014	AF	XRA A	Clear A register
4015	2C	INR L	Increment L register
4016	7D	MOV A, L	Move L register to A register
4017	FE	CPI 60H	Compare accumulator with 60H

4018	60		
4019	C2	JNZ **4003H**	Jump to 4003H until the zero flag is set
401A	03		
401B	40		
401C	AF	XRA A	Clear A register
401D	24	INR H	Increment H register
401E	7C	MOV A, H	Move H register to A register
401F	FE	CPI 24H	Compare accumulator with 24H
4020	24		
4021	C2	JNZ **4003H**	Jump to 4003H until the zero flag is set
4022	03		
4023	40		
4024	C3	JMP **4000H**	Jump to 4000H
4025	04		
4026	00		
Delay1s:			
4050	0E	MVI C, 02H	Move 02H to C register
4051	02		
4052	11	LXI D,FFFFH	Load FFFFH to D-E register pair
4053	FF		
4054	FF		
4055	1B	DCX D	Decrement D-E register pair
4056	7A	MOV A, D	Move D register to A register
4057	B3	ORA E	OR accumulator with E register
4058	C2	JNZ **4055H**	Jump to 4055H until the zero flag is set
4059			

405A			
405B	0D	DCR C	Decrement C register
405C	C2		
405D		JNZ **4052H**	Jump to 4052H until the zero flag is set
405E			
405F	C9	RET	Return to the main program

Experimental:

Address	H : M : S
5000	00 (M)
5001	00 (H)
5002	00 (S)

Conclusion:

Thus the assembly language program for the real-time clock using 8085 microprocessor has been simulated.

*****

Chapter - 2

8051 MICROCONTROLLER LABORATORY

2.1 Introduction to 8051 Microcontroller

A microcontroller is a digital computer manufactured on a single chip. The microcontroller contains a CPU, ROM, RAM, Clock circuit, Input-Output ports, Programmable timers/counters, Serial port, Interrupt handler, etc. Microcontrollers are usually dedicated devices that are embedded with the control systems. Therefore it is also called embedded controllers. In addition to the microcontroller, a complete embedded control system incorporates applications specific software, external memories, and application-specific hardware.

The 8051 microcontroller is the first most popular MCU of the MCS-51 family introduced by Intel Corporation in the 1980s. The 8051 Microcontroller is an 8-bit Microcontroller. It is built with 40 pins Plastic Dual Inline Package. The system bus composes of an 8-bit data bus and a 16-bit address bus. The microcontroller has various on-chip peripheral devices like 4kB of ROM storage, 128 bytes of RAM storage, two 16-bit timers, four parallel 8-bit ports, interrupt controller and universal asynchronous receiver transmitter. Figure 2.1 shows the simple internal architecture of an 8051 Microcontroller.

Figure 2.2 shows the pin diagram of an 8051 Microcontroller. The pin description of 8051 microcontroller as follows,

Pins 1 to 8: They are Port 1, bi-directional 8-bit I/O ports. It is internally pulled up.

Pin 9: It is a RESET pin, which is used to reset the microcontroller.

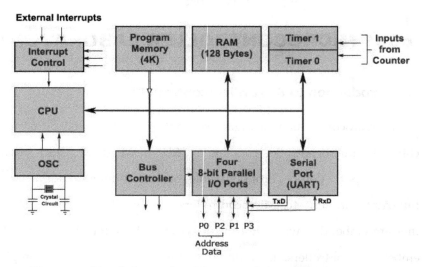

Figure 2.1. Simple internal architecture of an 8051 Microcontroller

Pins 10 to 17: They are Port 3, bi-directional 8-bit I/O ports. This port serves some other functions.

- o   Pin10 – RxD
- o   Pin11 – TxD
- o   Pin12 – INT0 (Active low signal)
- o   Pin13 – INT1 (Active low signal)
- o   Pin14 – T0
- o   Pin15 – T1

   o   Pin16 – WR (Active low signal)

   o   Pin17 – RD (Active low signal)

Pins 18 & 19: XTAL 1 and XTAL 2 which are used to receive the system clock inputs from the crystal clock circuit. The crystal frequency varies from 4MHz to 30 MHz, normally 11.0592 MHz crystal is used.

Pin 20: GND pin. The power supply ground.

Pins 21 to 28: They are Port 2, bi-directional 8-bit I/O ports. Higher-order address bus signals are multiplexed with this port (A8-A15).

Pin 29: This is PSEN (Program Store Enable) pin. It is used to read a signal from the external program memory.

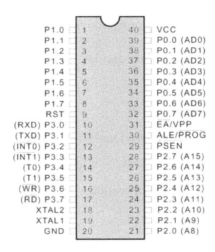

Figure 2.2. Pin diagram of 8051 Microcontroller

Pin 30: This is EA (External Access) input pin. It is used to enable/ disable the external memory interfacing.

Pin 31: This is ALE (Address Latch Enable) pin. It is used to de-multiplex the address-data signal of port 0.

Pins 32 to 39: They are Port 0, bi-directional 8-bit I/O ports. Lower order address and data bus signals are multiplexed with this port (AD0-AD7). The external pull-up resistors are required to operate this port as I/O.

Pin 40: Vcc pin, main power source. Normally it is connected with +5V DC.

The 8051 Microcontroller incorporates five interrupts. They are,

- o   INT0 – External Hardware Interrupt.
- o   TF0 – Timer 0 Overflow Interrupt.
- o   INT1 – External Hardware Interrupt.
- o   TF1 – Timer 1 Overflow Interrupt.
- o   R1/T1 – Serial communication Interrupt.

The 8051 MCU instructions are divided into five functional groups:

- o   Arithmetic operations
- o   Logical operations
- o   Boolean variable operations
- o   Data transfer operations
- o   Program branching operations

Arithmetic Operations

ADD	A,Rn	Add register to accumulator
ADD	A,direct	Add direct byte to accumulator
ADD	A, @Ri	Add indirect RAM to accumulator
ADD	A,#data	Add immediate data to accumulator
ADDC	A,Rn	Add register to accumulator with carry flag
ADDC	A,direct	Add direct byte to A with carry flag
ADDC	A, @Ri	Add indirect RAM to A with carry flag
ADDC	A, #data	Add immediate data to A with carry flag
SUBB	A,Rn	Subtract register from A with borrow
SUBB	A,direct	Subtract direct byte from A with borrow
SUBB	A,@Ri	Subtract indirect RAM from A with borrow
SUBB	A,#data	Subtract immediate data from A with borrow
INC	A	Increment accumulator
INC	Rn	Increment register
INC	direct	Increment direct byte
INC	@Ri	Increment indirect RAM
DEC	A	Decrement accumulator
DEC	Rn	Decrement register
DEC	direct	Decrement direct byte
DEC	@Ri	Decrement indirect RAM
INC	DPTR	Increment data pointer
MUL	AB	Multiply A and B
DIV	AB	Divide A by B
DA	A	Decimal adjust accumulator

Logic Operations

ANL	A,Rn	AND register to accumulator
ANL	A,direct	AND direct byte to accumulator
ANL	A,@Ri	AND indirect RAM to accumulator
ANL	A,#data	AND immediate data to accumulator
ANL	direct,A	AND accumulator to direct byte
ANL	direct,#data	AND immediate data to direct byte
ORL	A,Rn	OR register to accumulator
ORL	A,direct	OR direct byte to accumulator
ORL	A,@Ri	OR indirect RAM to accumulator
ORL	A,#data	OR immediate data to accumulator
ORL	direct,A	OR accumulator to direct byte
ORL	direct,#data	OR immediate data to direct byte
XRL	A,Rn	Exclusive OR register to accumulator
XRL	A direct	Exclusive OR direct byte to accumulator
XRL	A,@Ri	Exclusive OR indirect RAM to accumulator
XRL	A,#data	Exclusive OR immediate data to accumulator
XRL	direct,A	Exclusive OR accumulator to direct byte
XRL	direct,#data	Exclusive OR immediate data to direct byte
CLR	A	Clear accumulator
CPL	A	Complement accumulator
RL	A	Rotate accumulator left
RLC	A	Rotate accumulator left through carry
RR	A	Rotate accumulator right
RRC	A	Rotate accumulator right through carry
SWAP	A	Swap nibbles within the accumulator

Boolean Variable Manipulation

CLR	C	Clear carry flag
CLR	bit	Clear direct bit
SETB	C	Set carry flag
SETB	bit	Set direct bit
CPL	C	Complement carry flag
CPL	bit	Complement direct bit
ANL	C,bit	AND direct bit to carry flag
ANL	C,/bit	AND complement of direct bit to carry
ORL	C,bit	OR direct bit to carry flag
ORL	C,/bit	OR complement of direct bit to carry
MOV	C,bit	Move direct bit to carry flag
MOV	bit,C	Move carry flag to direct bit

Data Transfer

MOV	A,Rn	Move register to accumulator
MOV	A,direct [*]	Move direct byte to accumulator
MOV	A,@Ri	Move indirect RAM to accumulator
MOV	A,#data	Move immediate data to accumulator
MOV	Rn,A	Move accumulator to register
MOV	Rn,direct	Move direct byte to register
MOV	Rn,#data	Move immediate data to register
MOV	direct,A	Move accumulator to direct byte
MOV	direct,Rn	Move register to direct byte
MOV	direct,direct	Move direct byte to direct byte
MOV	direct,@Ri	Move indirect RAM to direct byte
MOV	direct,#data	Move immediate data to direct byte
MOV	@Ri,A	Move accumulator to indirect RAM
MOV	@Ri,direct	Move direct byte to indirect RAM
MOV	@Ri, #data	Move immediate data to indirect RAM
MOV	DPTR, #data16	Load data pointer with a 16-bit constant
MOVC	A,@A + DPTR	Move code byte relative to DPTR to accumulator
MOVC	A,@A + PC	Move code byte relative to PC to accumulator
MOVX	A,@Ri	Move external RAM (8-bit addr.) to A
MOVX	A,@DPTR	Move external RAM (16-bit addr.) to A
MOVX	@Ri,A	Move A to external RAM (8-bit addr.)
MOVX	@DPTR,A	Move A to external RAM (16-bit addr.)
PUSH	direct	Push direct byte onto stack
POP	direct	Pop direct byte from stack
XCH	A,Rn	Exchange register with accumulator
XCH	A,direct	Exchange direct byte with accumulator
XCH	A,@Ri	Exchange indirect RAM with accumulator
XCHD	A,@Ri	Exchange low-order nibble indir. RAM with A

Program and Machine Control

ACALL addr11	Absolute subroutine call
LCALL addr16	Long subroutine call
RET	Return from subroutine
RETI	Return from interrupt
AJMP addr11	Absolute jump
LJMP addr16	Long iump
SJMP rel	Short jump (relative addr.)
JMP @A + DPTR	Jump indirect relative to the DPTR
JZ rel	Jump if accumulator is zero
JNZ rel	Jump if accumulator is not zero
JC rel	Jump if carry flag is set
JNC rel	Jump if carry flag is not set
JB bit,rel	Jump if direct bit is set
JNB bit,rel	Jump if direct bit is not set
JBC bit,rel	Jump if direct bit is set and clear bit
CJNE A,direct,rel	Compare direct byte to A and jump if not equal

CJNE A,#data,rel	Compare immediate to A and jump if not equal
CJNE Rn,#data rel	Compare immed. to reg. and jump if not equal
CJNE @Ri,#data,rel	Compare immed. to ind. and jump if not equal
DJNZ Rn,rel	Decrement register and jump if not zero
DJNZ direct,rel	Decrement direct byte and jump if not zero
NOP	No operation

8051 Microcontroller Programming Tools

- The *EdSim51DI* Simulator and *Keil μVision IDE* are used for studying results of the 8051 assembly language programs.
- The *Keil μVision IDE* is a powerful and efficient tool which is used for an 8051 Embedded C programming.

2.2	ADDITION OF TWO 8-BIT NUMBERS

Aim:

Write an 8051 assembly language program to perform the addition of two 8-bit numbers.

Apparatus:

    o   8051 Microcontroller Trainer

Software Required:

    o   EdSim51DI Simulator/ Keil µVision IDE / any other supportive tool

Algorithm:

1. Initialize the carry value as zero in the R2 register
2. Move 5000H to DPTR for getting input values
3. Move the first operand into the accumulator
4. Keep the first operand in the R0 register
5. Increment the DPTR to get the next operand
6. Keep the second operand in the accumulator
7. Perform the addition operation
8. If the carry is not set, jump to step 10
9. Increment the R2 register for carry
10. Increment the DPTR and store the sum value
11. Increment the DPTR and store the carry value
12. Stop the program

Program:

Memory address	Label	Mnemonics & Operand(s)	Comments
4000		MOV R2, #00H	R2 = 00H
4002		MOV DPTR, #5000H	DPTR = 5000H
4005		MOVX A, @DPTR	A = [5000H]

4006		MOV R0, A	R0 = A
4007		INC DPTR	DPTR = 5001H
4008		MOVX A, @DPTR	A = [5001H]
4009		ADD A, R0	A = A + R0
400A		JNC **FRD**	Jump to 400EH if no carry
400D		INC R2	R2 = R2 + 1
400E	**FRD:**	INC DPTR	DPTR = 5002H
400F		MOVX @DPTR, A	[5002H] = A
4010		INC DPTR	DPTR = 5003H
4011		MOV A, R2	A = R2
4012		MOVX @DPTR, A	[5003H] = A
4013	**HLT:**	SJMP **HLT**	Stop the program

Experimental Results:

Input Data		Result	
Memory location	Operand	Memory location	Operand
5000	85 H	5002	2B H (sum)
5001	A6 H	5003	01 H (carry)

Calculation:

I/O	in HEX		in Binary		
Operand 1	85 H			1000	0101
Operand 2	A6 H			1010	0110
Result (carry & sum)	12B H		1	0010	1011

Conclusion:

The addition of two 8-bit numbers has been performed using the 8051 Microcontroller.

2.3	SUBTRACTION OF TWO 8-BIT NUMBERS

Aim:

Write an 8051 assembly language program to perform the subtraction of two 8-bit numbers.

Apparatus:

o   8051 Microcontroller Trainer

Software Required:

o   EdSim51DI Simulator/ Keil μVision IDE / any other supportive tool

Algorithm:

1. Initialize the borrow value as zero in R2 register
2. Move 5000H to DPTR for getting input values
3. Move the first operand (minuend) into the accumulator
4. Keep the first operand in the R0 register
5. Increment the DPTR to get the next operand
6. Keep the second operand (Subtrahend) in the accumulator
7. Move the accumulator to R1 register
8. Move the value of R0 register to the accumulator
9. Perform the subtraction operation (A=A-R1-B)
10. If the carry is not set, jump to step 12
11. Increment the R2 register for carry
12. Increment the DPTR and store the difference value
13. Increment the DPTR and store the borrow value
14. Stop the program

Program:

Memory address	Label	Mnemonics & Operand(s)	Comments
4000		MOV R2, #00H	R2 = 00H
4002		MOV DPTR, #5000H	DPTR = 5000H

4005		MOVX A, @DPTR	A = [5000H]
4006		MOV R0, A	R0 = A
4007		INC DPTR	DPTR = 5001H
4008		MOVX A, @DPTR	A = [5001H]
4009		MOV R1, A	R1 = A
400A		MOV A, R0	A = R0
400B		SUBB A, R1	A = A - R1 - B
400C		JNC **FRD**	Jump to 4010H if no carry
400F		INC R2	R2 = R2 + 1
4010	**FRD:**	INC DPTR	DPTR = 5002H
4011		MOVX @DPTR, A	[5002H] = A
4012		INC DPTR	DPTR = 5003H
4013		MOV A, R2	A = R2
4014		MOVX @DPTR, A	[5003H] = A
4015	**HLT:**	SJMP **HLT**	Stop the program

Experimental Results:

Input Data		Result	
Memory location	Operand	Memory location	Operand
5000	56 H (minuend)	5002	32 H (difference)
5001	24 H (subtrahend)	5003	00 H (borrow)

Calculation:

I/O	in HEX		in Binary		
Minuend	56 H			0101	0110
Subtrahend	24 H			0010	0100
Result (borrow & difference)	32 H		0	0011	0010

Conclusion:

The subtraction of two 8-bit numbers has been performed using the 8051 Microcontroller.

2.4 | ADDITION OF N 8-BIT NUMBERS IN AN ARRAY

Aim:

Write an 8051 assembly language program to find the sum of N 8-bit numbers in an array.

Apparatus:

- o 8051 Microcontroller Trainer

Software Required:

- o EdSim51DI Simulator/ Keil µVision IDE / any other supportive tool

Algorithm:

1. Initialize the carry value as zero in the R3 register
2. Move 5000H to DPTR for getting input values
3. Move the number of data in an array into an accumulator
4. Move the accumulator to the R0 register. (Count)
5. Increment the DPTR to get the operand
6. Keep the operand in the R1 register
7. Decrement the count value at R0
8. Increment the DPTR to get the next operand
9. Keep the operand in the R2 register
10. Move the value of R1 to the accumulator
11. Perform the addition operation (A = A + R2)
12. If the carry is not set, jump to step 14
13. Increment the R3 register for carry
14. Move the accumulator to the R1 register
15. Decrement R0 and jump to step 8 if it is a non-zero value
16. Increment the DPTR and store the sum value

17. Increment the DPTR and store the carry value
18. Stop the program

Program:

Memory address	Label	Mnemonics & Operand(s)	Comments
4000		MOV R3, #00H	R3 = 00H (carry)
4002		MOV DPTR, #5000H	DPTR = 5000H
4005		MOVX A, @DPTR	A = [5000H]
4006		MOV R0, A	R0 = A (No of data)
4007		INC DPTR	DPTR = 5001H
4008		MOVX A, @DPTR	A = [5001H]
4009		MOV R1, A	R1 = A
400A		DEC R0	R0 = R0 - 1
400B	**BK:**	INC DPTR	DPTR = DPTR + 1
400C		MOVX A, @DPTR	A = [[DPTR]]
400D		MOV R2, A	R2 = A
400E		MOV A, R1	A = R1
400F		ADD A, R2	A = A + R2
4010		JNC **FRD**	Jump to 4014H if no carry
4013		INC R3	R3 = R3 + 1
4014	**FRD:**	MOV R1, A	R1 = A
4015		DJNZ R0, **BK**	Jump to 400BH if R0 is not equal to zero
4018		INC DPTR	DPTR = DPTR + 1
4019		MOVX @DPTR, A	[[DPTR]] = A
401A		INC DPTR	DPTR = DPTR + 1
401B		MOV A, R3	A = R2
401C		MOVX @DPTR, A	[[DPTR]] = A

401D	HLT:	SJMP HLT	Stop the program

Experimental Results:

Input Data		Result	
Memory location	Operand	Memory location	Operand
5000	04 H*	5005	74 H (sum)
5001	16 H	5006	01 H (carry)
5002	42 H	-	-
5003	73 H	-	-
5004	A9 H	-	-

* Number of array elements

Calculation:

I/O	in HEX
Count	04 H
Operand 1	16 H
Operand 2	42 H
Operand 3	73 H
Operand 4	38 H
Result	103 H

Conclusion:

The addition of N 8-bit numbers in an array has been performed using the 8051 Microcontroller.

2.5	MULTIPLICATION OF TWO 8-BIT NUMBERS

Aim:

Write an 8051 assembly language program to perform the multiplication of two 8-bit numbers.

Apparatus:

o   8051 Microcontroller Trainer

Software Required:

o   EdSim51DI Simulator/ Keil µVision IDE / any other supportive tool

Algorithm:

1.   Move 5000H to DPTR for getting input values
2.   Move the first operand (multiplicand) into the accumulator
3.   Keep the first operand in the R0 register
4.   Increment the DPTR to get the next operand
5.   Keep the second operand (multiplier) in the accumulator
6.   Move the accumulator to the B register
7.   Move the value of R0 to the accumulator
8.   Perform the multiplication operation (BA = A * B)
9.   Increment the DPTR and store the accumulator value (LSB of Product)
10. Increment the DPTR and store the B register value (MSB of Product)
11. Stop the program

Program:

Memory address	Label	Mnemonics & Operand(s)	Comments
4000		MOV DPTR, #5000H	DPTR = 5000H
4003		MOVX A, @DPTR	A = [5000H]
4004		MOV R0, A	R0 = A
4005		INC DPTR	DPTR = 5001H
4006		MOVX A, @DPTR	A = [5001H]
4007		MOV B, A	B = A

4008		MOV A, R0	A = R0
4009		MUL AB	BA = A * B
400A		INC DPTR	DPTR = 5002H
400B		MOVX @DPTR, A	[5002H] = A
400C		INC DPTR	DPTR = 5003H
400D		MOV A, B	A = B
400E		MOVX @DPTR, A	[5003H] = A
400F	**HLT:**	SJMP **HLT**	Stop the program

Experimental Results:

Input Data		Result	
Memory location	Operand	Memory location	Operand
5000	06 H	5002	18 H (Product-LSB)
5001	04 H	5003	00 H (Product-MSB)

Calculation:

I/O	in HEX
Multiplicand	06 H
Multiplier	04 H
Product 18H	Multiplicand x Multiplier 06H x 04H
Product (LSB)	18 H
Product (MSB)	00 H

Conclusion:

The multiplication of two 8-bit numbers has been performed using the 8051 Microcontroller.

2.6	DIVISION OF TWO 8-BIT NUMBERS

Aim:

Write an 8051 assembly language program to perform the division of two 8-bit numbers.

Apparatus:

- o   8051 Microcontroller Trainer

Software Required:

- o   EdSim51DI Simulator/ Keil µVision IDE / any other supportive tool

Algorithm:

1. Move 5000H to DPTR for getting input values
2. Move the first operand (Dividend) into the accumulator
3. Keep the first operand in the R0 register
4. Increment the DPTR to get the next operand
5. Keep the second operand (Divisor) in the accumulator
6. Move the accumulator to the B register
7. Move the value of R0 to the accumulator
8. Perform the division operation (BA = A / B)
9. Increment the DPTR and store the accumulator value (Quotient)
10. Increment the DPTR and store the B register value (Remainder)
11. Stop the program

Program:

Memory address	Label	Mnemonics & Operand(s)	Comments
4000		MOV DPTR, #5000H	DPTR = 5000H
4003		MOVX A, @DPTR	A = [5000H]
4004		MOV R0, A	R0 = A (Dividend)

4005		INC DPTR	DPTR = 5001H
4006		MOVX A, @DPTR	A = [5001H]
4007		MOV B, A	B = A (Divisor)
4008		MOV A, R0	A = R0
4009		DIV AB	A = A / B (Remainder in B)
400A		INC DPTR	DPTR = 5002H
400B		MOVX @DPTR, A	[5002H] = A (Quotient)
400C		INC DPTR	DPTR = 5003H
400D		MOV A, B	A = B
400E		MOVX @DPTR, A	[5003H] = A (Remainder)
400F	HLT:	SJMP HLT	Stop the program

Experimental Results:

Input Data		Result	
Memory location	Operand	Memory location	Operand
5000	19 H	5002	08 H (quotient)
5001	03 H	5003	01 H (remainder)

Calculation:

I/O	in HEX
Dividend	19 H
Divisor	03 H
Quotient	Dividend / Divisor 19H / 03H
Quotient	08 H
Remainder	01 H

Conclusion:

The division of two 8-bit numbers has been performed using the 8051 Microcontroller.

2.7	LARGEST NUMBER IN AN ARRAY

Aim:

Write an 8051 assembly language program to find the largest number in an 8-bit array.

Apparatus:

- o   8051 Microcontroller Trainer

Software Required:

- o   EdSim51DI Simulator/ Keil μVision IDE / any other supportive tool

Algorithm:

1. Move 5000H to DPTR for getting input values.
2. Clear carry
3. Move the first value to R0 (it is a number of bytes in an array).
4. Increment the DPTR
5. Keep this value in RAM address 20H. (It holds the larger value always)
6. Decrement R0
7. Increment the DPTR and hold the value in the accumulator
8. Compare accumulator and the content of 20H, jump to step 10 if they are not equal
9. Jump to step 12
10. Jump to step 12 if carry is set
11. Move the accumulator to 20H
12. Decrement R0, jump to step 7 until the non-zero value in R0
13. Increment DPTR
14. Move the content of 20H to the accumulator
15. Move the result to the memory location which is pointed by DPTR.
16. Stop the program

Program:

Memory address	Label	Mnemonics & Operand(s)	Comments
4000		MOV DPTR, #5000H	DPTR = 5000H
4003		CLR C	Clear carry
4004		MOVX A, @DPTR	A = [[DPTR]]
4005		MOV R0, A	R0 = A
4006		INC DPTR	DPTR = DPTR + 1
4007		MOVX A, @DPTR	A = [[DPTR]]
4008		MOV 20H, A	[20H] = A
400A		DEC R0	R0 = R0 - 1
400B	**FD:**	INC DPTR	DPTR = DPTR + 1
400C		MOVX A, @DPTR	A = [[DPTR]]
400D		CJNE A, 20H, **TN**	A – [20H], if not equal, jump to TN
4010		SJMP **NEXT**	Short jump to NEXT
4013	**TN:**	JC **NEXT**	Jump to NEXT if carry is set
4016		MOV 20H, A	[20H] = A
4018	**NEXT:**	DJNZ R0, **FD**	R0 = R0 – 1 Jump to FD if non-zero
401B		INC DPTR	DPTR = DPTR + 1
401C		MOV A, 20H	A = [20H]
401E		MOVX @DPTR, A	[[DPTR]] = A
401F	**HLT:**	SJMP **HLT**	Short jump to HLT

Experimental Results:

Input Data		Result	
Memory location	Operand	Memory location	Operand
5000	05 H	5006	CA H
5001	56 H	-	-
5002	98 H	-	-
5003	12 H	-	-
5004	CA H	-	-
5005	75 H	-	-

* 5000H having number of bytes in an array

Conclusion:

The 8051 assembly language program for finding largest number of an 8-bit array has been executed and the result is stored in the memory location 5006H.

2.8	SMALLEST NUMBER IN AN ARRAY

Aim:

Write an 8051 assembly language program to find the smallest number in an 8-bit array.

Apparatus:

o   8051 Microcontroller Trainer

Software Required:

o   EdSim51DI Simulator/ Keil μVision IDE / any other supportive tool

Algorithm:

1.   Move 5000H to DPTR for getting input values

2. Clear carry

3. Move the first value to R0 (it is a number of bytes in an array).

4. Increment the DPTR

5. Keep this value in RAM address 20H. (It holds the smaller value always)

6. Decrement R0

7. Increment the DPTR and hold the value in the accumulator

8. Compare accumulator and the content of 20H, jump to step 10 if they are not equal

9. Jump to step 12

10. Jump to step 12 for no carry

11. Move the accumulator to 20H

12. Decrement R0, jump to step 7 until the non-zero value in R0

13. Increment DPTR

14. Move the content of 20H to the accumulator

15. Move the result to the memory location which is pointed by DPTR

16. Stop the program

Program:

Memory address	Label	Mnemonics & Operand(s)	Comments
4000		MOV DPTR, #5000H	DPTR = 5000H
4003		CLR C	Clear carry
4004		MOVX A, @DPTR	A = [[DPTR]]
4005		MOV R0, A	R0 = A
4006		INC DPTR	DPTR = DPTR + 1
4007		MOVX A, @DPTR	A = [[DPTR]]
4008		MOV 20H, A	[20H] = A
400A		DEC R0	R0 = R0 - 1
400B	FD:	INC DPTR	DPTR = DPTR + 1
400C		MOVX A, @DPTR	A = [[DPTR]]

400D		CJNE A, 20H, **TN**	A – [20H], if not equal, jump to TN
4010		SJMP **NEXT**	Short jump to NEXT
4013	**TN:**	JNC **NEXT**	Jump to NEXT for no carry
4016		MOV 20H, A	[20H] = A
4018	**NEXT:**	DJNZ R0, **FD**	R0 = R0 – 1 Jump to FD if non-zero
401B		INC DPTR	DPTR = DPTR + 1
401C		MOV A, 20H	A = [20H]
401E		MOVX @DPTR, A	[[DPTR]] = A
401F	**HLT:**	SJMP **HLT**	Short jump to HLT

Experimental Results:

Input Data		Result	
Memory location	Operand	Memory location	Operand
5000	05 H	5006	12 H
5001	56 H	-	-
5002	98 H	-	-
5003	12 H	-	-
5004	CA H	-	-
5005	75 H	-	-

* 5000H having number of bytes in an array

Conclusion:

The 8051 assembly language program for finding smallest number of an 8-bit array has been executed and the result is stored in the memory location 5006H.

2.9	DESCENDING ORDER OF AN ARRAY

Aim:

Write an 8051 assembly language program to arrange the bytes in an array in descending order.

Apparatus:

o   8051 Microcontroller Trainer

Software Required:

o   EdSim51DI Simulator/ Keil μVision IDE / any other supportive tool

Algorithm:

1.   Move number of bytes in an array to R7

2.   Move number of bytes in an array to R6

3.   Move 5000H to DPTR for getting input values

4.   Clear carry

5.   Move the content pointed by the DPTR to R1

6.   Increment the DPTR

7.   Get the next byte at an accumulator

8.   Subtract R1 with borrow from the accumulator

9.   Jump to step 16 if carry is set

10. Move the content pointed by the DPTR to the accumulator

11. Decrement DPL

12. Move the accumulator to a memory location which is pointed by the DPTR

13. Move R1 to the accumulator

14. Increment DPL

15. Move the accumulator to a memory location which is pointed by the DPTR

16. Decrement R6, jump to step 5 until R6 equal to zero

17. Decrement R7, jump to step 2 until R7 equal to zero

18. Stop the program

Program:

Memory address	Label	Mnemonics & Operand(s)	Comments
4000		MOV R7, #05H	R7 = 05H (no. of bytes in an array)
4003	**AGN:**	MOV R6, #05H	R5 = 05H (no. of bytes in an array)
4004		MOV DPTR, #5000H	DPTR = 5000H
4005		CLR C	Clear carry
4006	**FRD:**	MOVX A, @DPTR	A = [[DPTR]]
4007		MOV R1, A	R1 = A
4008		INC DPTR	DPTR = DPTR + 1
400A		MOVX A, @DPTR	A = [[DPTR]]
400B		SUBB A, R1	A = A – R1 - B
400C		JC **SKP**	Jump to SKP if carry is set
400D		MOVX A, @DPTR	A = [[DPTR]]
4010		DEC DPL	DPL = DPL - 1
4013		MOVX @DPTR, A	[[DPTR]] = A
4016		MOV A, R1	A = R1
4018		INC DPL	DPH = DPH + 1
401B		MOVX @DPTR, A	[[DPTR]] = A
401C	**SKP:**	DJNZ R6, **FRD**	R6 = R6 -1 Jump to FRD until R6 = 0
401E		DJNZ R7, **AGN**	R7 = R7 -1 Jump to AGN until R7 = 0
401F	**HLT:**	SJMP **HLT**	Short jump to HLT

Experimental Results:

Input Data		Result	
Memory location	Operand	Memory location	Operand

5000	56 H	5000	CA H
5001	98 H	5001	98 H
5002	12 H	5002	75 H
5003	CA H	5003	56 H
5004	75 H	5004	12 H
5005	09 H	5005	09 H

Conclusion:

The 8051 assembly language program for arranging the bytes of an array in descending order has been executed.

2.10	ASCENDING ORDER OF AN ARRAY

Aim:

Write an 8051 assembly language program to arrange the bytes in an array in ascending order.

Apparatus:

o   8051 Microcontroller Trainer

Software Required:

o   EdSim51DI Simulator/ Keil μVision IDE / any other supportive tool

Algorithm:

1.   Move number of bytes in an array to R7
2.   Move number of bytes in an array to R6
3.   Move 5000H to DPTR for getting input values
4.   Clear carry
5.   Move the content pointed by the DPTR to R1
6.   Increment the DPTR
7.   Get the next byte at an accumulator
8.   Subtract R1 with borrow from the accumulator

9. Jump to step 16 if no carry
10. Move the content pointed by the DPTR to the accumulator
11. Decrement DPL
12. Move the accumulator to a memory location which is pointed by the DPTR
13. Move R1 to the accumulator
14. Increment DPL
15. Move the accumulator to a memory location which is pointed by the DPTR
16. Decrement R6, jump to step 5 until R6 equal to zero
17. Decrement R7, jump to step 2 until R7 equal to zero
18. Stop the program

Program:

Memory address	Label	Mnemonics & Operand(s)	Comments
4000		MOV R7, #05H	R7 = 05H (no. of bytes in an array)
4003	**AGN:**	MOV R6, #05H	R5 = 05H (no. of bytes in an array)
4004		MOV DPTR, #5000H	DPTR = 5000H
4005		CLR C	Clear carry
4006	**FRD:**	MOVX A, @DPTR	A = [[DPTR]]
4007		MOV R1, A	R1 = A
4008		INC DPTR	DPTR = DPTR + 1
400A		MOVX A, @DPTR	A = [[DPTR]]
400B		SUBB A, R1	A = A – R1 - B
400C		JNC **SKP**	Jump to SKP if no carry
400D		MOVX A, @DPTR	A = [[DPTR]]
4010		DEC DPL	DPL = DPL - 1
4013		MOVX @DPTR, A	[[DPTR]] = A

4016		MOV A, R1	A = R1
4018		INC DPL	DPH = DPH + 1
401B		MOVX @DPTR, A	[[DPTR]] = A
401C	**SKP:**	DJNZ R6, **FRD**	R6 = R6 -1 Jump to FRD until R6 = 0
401E		DJNZ R7, **AGN**	R7 = R7 -1 Jump to AGN until R7 = 0
401F	**HLT:**	SJMP **HLT**	Short jump to HLT

Experimental Results:

Input Data		Result	
Memory location	Operand	Memory location	Operand
5000	56 H	5000	09 H
5001	98 H	5001	12 H
5002	12 H	5002	56 H
5003	CA H	5003	75 H
5004	75 H	5004	98 H
5005	09 H	5005	CA H

Conclusion:

The 8051 assembly language program for arranging the bytes of an array in ascending order has been executed.

| 2.11 | LOGICAL OPERATIONS |

Aim:

Write an 8051 assembly language program to perform the logical operations of 8-bit numbers.

Apparatus:

o   8051 Microcontroller Trainer

Software Required:

o   EdSim51DI Simulator/ Keil µVision IDE / any other supportive tool

Algorithm:

1. Move 5000H to DPTR for getting input values
2. Move the first operand into the accumulator
3. Keep the first operand in the R0 register
4. Increment the DPTR to get the next operand
5. Keep the second operand in the accumulator
6. Move the accumulator to the R1 register
7. Move the value of R0 to the accumulator
8. Perform the AND operation (A = A AND R1)
9. Increment the DPTR and store AND result
10. Move the value of R0 to the accumulator
11. Perform the OR operation (A = A OR R1)
12. Increment the DPTR and store OR result
13. Move the value of R0 to the accumulator
14. Perform the XOR operation (A = A XOR R1)
15. Increment the DPTR and store XOR result
16. Move the value of R0 to the accumulator
17. Perform the NOT operation (A = NOT A)
18. Increment the DPTR and store NOT result
19. Stop the program

Program:

Memory address	Label	Mnemonics & Operand(s)	Comments
4000		MOV DPTR, #5000H	DPTR = 5000H
4003		MOVX A, @DPTR	A = [5000H]

4004		MOV R0, A	R0 = A
4005		INC DPTR	DPTR = 5001H
4006		MOVX A, @DPTR	A = [5001H]
4007		MOV R1, A	R1 = A
4008		MOV A, R0	A = R0
4009		ANL A, R1	A = A AND R1
400A		INC DPTR	DPTR = 5002H
400B		MOVX @DPTR, A	[5002H] = A
400C		MOV A, R0	A = R0
400D		ORL A, R1	A = A OR R1
400E		INC DPTR	DPTR = 5003H
400F		MOVX @DPTR, A	[5003H] = A
4010		MOV A, R0	A = R0
4011		XRL A, R1	A = A XOR R1
4012		INC DPTR	DPTR = 5004H
4013		MOVX @DPTR, A	[5004H] = A
4014		MOV A, R0	A = R0
4015		CPL A	A = NOT (A)
4016		INC DPTR	DPTR = 5005H
4017		MOVX @DPTR, A	[5005H] = A
4018	HLT:	SJMP HLT	Stop the program

Experimental Results:

Input Data		Result	
Memory location	Operand	Memory location	Operand
5000	A5 H	5002	21 H (AND)
5001	63 H	5003	E7 H (OR)
-	-	5004	C6 H (XOR)
-	-	5005	5A H (~A)

Calculation:

I/O	in Binary	in HEX
Operand 1	1010 0101	A5 H
Operand 2	0110 0011	63 H
AND	0010 0001	21 H
OR	1110 0111	E7 H
XOR	1100 0110	C6 H
~ A	0101 1010	5A H

Conclusion:

The logical operations of two 8-bit numbers have been performed using the 8051 Microcontroller.

2.12	VERIFICATION OF DEMORGAN'S THEOREM

Aim:

Write an 8051 assembly language program to verify the Demorgan's theorem.

Apparatus:

o   8051 Microcontroller Trainer

Software Required:

o   EdSim51DI Simulator/ Keil μVision IDE / any other supportive tool

Algorithm:

The Demorgan's theorem is

$$\overline{A.B} = \overline{A} + \overline{B}$$

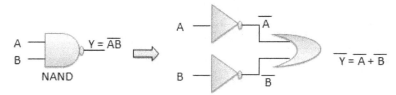

- LHS represents NAND of A and B.
- RHS represents OR of inverted inputs.

1. Move 5000H to DPTR for getting input values
2. Move the first operand into the accumulator
3. Keep the first operand in the R0 register
4. Increment the DPTR to get the next operand
5. Keep the second operand in the accumulator
6. Move the accumulator to the R1 register
7. Move the value of R0 to the accumulator
8. Perform the AND operation (A = A AND R1)
9. Perform the NOT operation (A = NOT A)
10. Increment the DPTR and store LHS result
11. Move the value of R1 to the accumulator
12. Perform the NOT operation (A = NOT A)
13. Move the accumulator to R1 register
14. Move the value of R0 to the accumulator
15. Perform the NOT operation (A = NOT A)
16. Perform the OR operation (A = A OR R1)
17. Increment the DPTR and store RHS result
18. Stop the program

Program:

Memory address	Label	Mnemonics & Operand(s)	Comments
4000		MOV DPTR, #5000H	DPTR = 5000H
4003		MOVX A, @DPTR	A = [5000H]

4004		MOV R0, A	R0 = A
4005		INC DPTR	DPTR = 5001H
4006		MOVX A, @DPTR	A = [5001H]
4007		MOV R1, A	R1 = A
4008		MOV A, R0	A = R0
4009		ANL A, R1	A = A AND R1
400A		CPL A	A = NOT (A)
400B		INC DPTR	DPTR = 5002H
400C		MOVX @DPTR, A	[5002H] = A
400D		MOV A, R1	A = R1
400E		CPL A	A = NOT (A)
400F		MOV R1, A	R1 = A
4010		MOV A, R0	A = R0
4011		CPL A	A = NOT (A)
4012		ORL A, R1	A = A OR R1
4013		INC DPTR	DPTR = 5003H
4014		MOVX @DPTR, A	[5003H] = A
4015	**HLT:**	SJMP **HLT**	Stop the program

Experimental Results:

Input Data		Result	
Memory location	Operand	Memory location	Operand
5000	13 H	5002	EE H (LHS)
5001	75 H	5003	EE H (RHS)

Calculation:

I/O	in Binary	in HEX
Operand 1	0001 0011	13H
Operand 2	0111 0101	75H

LHS		
AND	0001 0001	11H
AND BAR	1110 1110	EEH
RHS		
A BAR	1110 1100	ECH
B BAR	1000 1010	8AH
A BAR + B BAR	1110 1110	EEH

Conclusion:

The Demorgan's theorem has been verified using the 8051 Microcontroller.

2.13	SQUARE WAVE GENERATION USING SOFTWARE TIME DELAY

Aim:

1. Write an 8051 assembly language program to generate 2500 Hz square wave signal at port 1.0 using 8051 software delay.
2. Write an 8051 Embedded C program to generate 1 kHz square wave signal at port 1.0 using 8051 software delay.

Apparatus:

o   8051 Microcontroller board

Software Required:

o   EdSim51DI Simulator/ Keil μVision IDE / any other supportive tool

Theory:

Time delay generation is one of the important concepts dealing with the Microcontrollers and it is used in almost all microcontroller applications.

There are two ways to generate a time delay

- Time delay using software
- Time delay using an on-chip timer

The following factors should be considered during the calculation of time delay using software

- Crystal oscillator connected to 8051 MCU.
- To calculate the machine cycle or instruction cycle of the system.
- Number of machine cycles for each instruction

Crystal oscillator: The frequency of the crystal connected to the 8051 family can vary from 4 MHz to 30 MHz, depending on the chip.

Machine cycles: CPU executing an instruction takes a certain number of clock cycles.

In 8051, one machine cycle takes 12 oscillator periods.

The length of machine cycle depends on the frequency of the crystal oscillator connected to 8051.

Find the machine cycle of 8051 for the following crystals

11.0592 MHz: 11.0592/12 = 921.6 KHz

Machine cycle = 1/921.6 KHz = 1.085us [us=microsecond]

20MHz: 20MHz/12 = 1.66 MHz

Machine Cycle = 1/1.66 MHz = 0.60us

Instructions – Execution time:

Instruction	Machine Cycle	Time To Execute
MOV R2, #55H	1	1 x 1.085 us = 1.085 us
DEC R2	1	1 x 1.085 us = 1.085 us
DJNZ R2, target	2	2 x 1.085 us = 2.17 us
LJMP label	2	2 x 1.085 us = 2.17 us

SJMP label	2	2 x 1.085 us = 2.17 us
NOP	1	1 x 1.085 us = 1.085 us

Example 1:

Find the size of the delay program - Single register delay subroutine

If a crystal frequency is 12 MHz, the machine cycle of a system is 1 us.

Delay Subroutine	No. of times execution	Machine Cycle	Total execution time
Delay: MOV R2, #255	1	1	1 x 1 x 1 us = 1 us
HR: DJNZ R2, HR	255	2	255 x 2 x 1 us = 510 us
RET	1	2	1 x 2 x 1 us = 2 us
Time delay			513 us

Time delay = [1 + 510 + 2] us = **513 us**

Note: NOP instruction is used to increase the delay in the loop.

Example 2:

Loop Inside a Loop Delay:

This method is used to get a larger time delay by implementing a loop inside a loop, which is also called a nested loop.

Delay Subroutine	No. of times execution	Machine Cycle	Total Time
Delay: MOV R2, # 66	1	1	1 x 1 x 1 us = 1 us
Again: MOV R3, #250	66	1	66 x 1 x 1 us = 66 us
HR: NOP	250 x 66	1	250 x66 x 1 x 1 us =16500 us
DJNZ R3, HR	250 x 66	2	250 x66 x 2 x 1 us =33000 us
DJNZ R2, Again	66	2	66 x 2 x 1 us = 132 us
RET	1	2	1 x 2 x 1 us = 2 us
Time delay			49.7 us = ~50 ms

Time delay = [1 + 66 + 16500 + 33000 + 132 + 2] us = 49701 us = **49.7 ms**

Algorithm:

Main:

1. Move 0x01 to port 1 (P1.0)
2. Call delay subroutine for 200 ms
3. Move 0x00 to port 1 (P1.0)
4. Call delay subroutine for 200 ms
5. Jump to step 1

Delay subroutine:

1. Load counter register (R2) with loop count (99)
2. Decrement counter register and jump back to the same instruction until the counter register value becomes zero
3. Return to the main program

Program:
Assembly language:

Label	Mnemonics & Operand(s)	Comments
	ORG 00H	Program starts from 0000H
	LJMP MAIN	Long jump to MAIN
	ORG 100H	Main source code starts from 100H
MAIN:	MOV P1, #0x01	Move 00000001 to PORT1
	CALL **Delay**	Call Delay Subroutine
	MOV P1, #0x00	Move 00000000 to PORT1
	CALL **Delay**	Call Delay Subroutine
	SJMP **MAIN**	Jump to MAIN
Delay:	MOV R2, #99	Load Register R2 with 99
Wait:	DJNZ R2, Wait	Decrement R2 till it is 0. Jump to Wait until R2 is non-zero
	RET	Return to main program

Embedded C language:

// 1 KHz square wave generation

```
#include<reg51.h>              // 8051 MCU header file inclusion
sbit LED = P1^0;               // Defining LED pin
void delay_ms (unsigned int);  // Function prototype declaration

void main (void)
{
    while(1)                   // infinite loop
    {
        LED = 0;               // LED ON
        delay_ms (1);          // Call delay function for 1ms
        LED = 1;               // LED OFF
        delay_ms (1);          // Call delay function for 1ms
    }
}
//delay in 1 millisecond for 11.0592MHz crystal
void delay_ms (unsigned int k)
{
unsigned int i, j;             // declaration of local variables
for(i=0; i<k; i++)             // for loop
  {
    for(j=0; j<110; j++);      // delay using for loop
  }
}
```

Experimental Results:

2500 Hz   **1 kHz**

Calculation:

Write a program for 200 us delay program.

If a crystal frequency is 12 MHz, the machine cycle of a system is 1 us.

Time delay = $[1 + 2*x + 2]$ us   (x is a loop count value)

200 us = $[3 + 2x]$ us

$3 + 2x = 200$

$2x = 200-3 = 197$

$x = 197/2 = 98.5 = $ **99 (decimal value)**

Delay Subroutine	No. of times execution	Machine Cycle	Total execution time
Delay: MOV R2, #99	1	1	$1 \times 1 \times 1$ us $= 1$ us
HR: DJNZ R2, HR	99	2	$99 \times 2 \times 1$ us $= 198$ us
RET	1	2	$1 \times 2 \times 1$ us $= 2$ us
Time delay			**201 us**

Frequency of square wave:

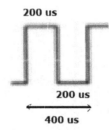

200 us

200 us

400 us

$F = 1/T = 1/400$ us $= 2500$ Hz

Conclusion:

The square wave signal has been generated with the frequency of 2500 Hz and 1 kHz using the 8051 Microcontroller.

2.14	LED BLINKING USING 8051 TIMER

Aim:

1. Write an 8051 assembly language program for blinking LED at port 1.0 using 8051 on-chip timer.
2. Write an 8051 Embedded C program to for blinking LED at port 1.0 using 8051 on-chip timer.

Apparatus:

o   8051 Microcontroller kit and LED

Software Required:

o   EdSim51DI Simulator/ Keil µVision IDE / any other supportive tool

Theory:

Embedded systems often require mechanisms for performing tasks at regular intervals and for counting the occurrence of events. The embedded processors are often equipped with hardware support for this functionality. It is called on-chip TIMER.

The timer used an internal clock of the microcontroller for its clock. A Timer is used for producing precise time delay. Counter use external clock, the external clock may come from a sensor to count the external events.

8051 has two timers/counters: Timer 0 and Timer 1. Both Timer 0 and Timer 1 are 16 bits wide. They can be used either as timers to generate a time delay or as counters to count events happening outside the microcontroller.

There are three registers in timer to control its operation
* Timer register: THx and TLx
  x is 0 or 1 for Timer 0 (TH0, TL0) and Timer 1 (TH1, TL1)
* Timer control register: TCON (8-bit)
* Timer mode register: TMOD (8-bit)

<u>Example 1:</u>

To generate **50 ms delay** using timer 0 in mode 1 of 8051 MCU.

Step 1:

Calculation of Timer 0 value needed to achieve timer delay of 50 ms.

If the oscillator frequency is 12 MHz. Timer clock = 12/12 MHz = 1 us

Delay Value   = Timer Delay / Timer Clock Cycle

$$= 50 \text{ ms} / 1 \text{ us}$$

$$= 50,000$$

Timer register value $\quad = 65,535 - 50,000$

$$= 15,535$$

$$= 0x3CAF$$

THO = 0x3C and TL0 = 0xAF

Step 2:

To find the value of TMOD register

Timer 0 in Mode 1

0	0	0	0	0	0	0	1

TMOD = 0x01

Step 3:

To start timer by setting TR0

To monitor TF0 flag bit.

If TF0 is set, clear TF0, and clear TR0 to stop the timer.

Algorithm:

Main:

1. Move 0x01 to port 2 (P2.0)
2. Call delay subroutine for 500 ms
3. Move 0x00 to port 2 (P2.0)
4. Call delay subroutine for 500 ms
5. Jump to step 1

Delay subroutine:

To generate time delay using the mode 1 of 8051 timer:

1. Load registers TL and TH with initial count values for required time delay

2. Load the TMOD value register indicating which timer (Timer 0 or Timer 1) is to be used and which timer mode is selected

3. Start the timer by setting TRx

4. Keep monitoring the timer flag (TF) with the instruction "JNB TFx, target". Get out of the loop when TF becomes high

5. Stop the timer by clearing TRx

6. Clear the TF flag

Program:

Assembly Language:

Label	Mnemonics & Operand(s)	Comments
	ORG 00H	Program starts from 0000H
	LJMP MAIN	Long jump to MAIN
	ORG 100H	Main source code starts from 100H
MAIN:	MOV P2, #0x01	Move 00000001 to PORT2
	CALL **Delay**	Call Delay Subroutine
	MOV P2, #0x00	Move 00000000 to PORT2
	CALL **Delay**	Call Delay Subroutine
	SJMP **MAIN**	Jump to MAIN
Delay:	MOV R1, #0x0A	Move count value to **R1** **10** x 50 ms = 500 ms
RPT:	MOV TH0, #0x3C	TH0 = 0x3C and TL0 = 0xAF
	MOV TL0, #0x0AF	
	MOV TMOD, #0x01	TMOD = 0x01
	SETB TR0	Start Timer0, TR0=1
Wait:	JNB TF0, **Wait**	Wait until the TF0 is set
	CLR TR0	Stop Timer0, TR0=0

	CLR TF0	Clear Timer0 flag, TF0=0
	DJNZ R1, RPT	Decrement count value (R1) and jump to RPT until R1=0
	RET	Return to main program
	END	End directive to suspend the program

Embedded C:

```
#include<reg51.h>              // 8051 MCU header file inclusion
sbit LED = P2^0;               // Defining LED pin
void delay1ms (unsigned int);  // Function prototype declaration
void main (void)
{
  while(1)                     // infinite loop
  {
    LED = 0;                   // LED ON
    delay1ms (500);            // Call delay function for 500 ms
    LED = 1;                   // LED OFF
    delay1ms (500);            // Call delay function for 500 ms
  }
}

// Timer0 mode 1- 1ms delay
void delay1ms (unsigned int t)
{
unsigned int i;
        for(i=0;i<t; i++)
        {
        TH0=0xfc;              // Timer register value for 1 ms
        TL0=0x66;
        TMOD=0x01;             // Timer 0 – mode 1
        TR0=1;                 // Start timer
        while(TF0==0);         // Wait until TF0 is set
        TR0=0;                 // Stop timer0
        TF0=0;                 // Clear Timer0 flag
        }
}
```

Experimental Result – Circuit Diagram:

Led blinking at Port 2.0.

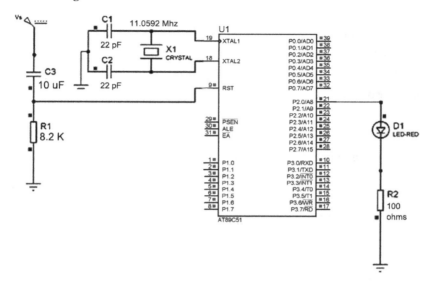

Conclusion:

The 8051 timer based assembly language and embedded C programs for LED blinking have been executed.

2.15	RING COUNTER

Aim:

1. Write an 8051 assembly language program for ring counter.
2. Write an 8051 Embedded C program for ring counter.

Apparatus:

○   8051 Microcontroller kit, 74LS245 and LEDs

Software Required:

○   Keil μVision IDE / EdSim51DI Simulator/ any other supportive tool

Algorithm:

1. Move 0x80 to port 2 (P2)
2. Call delay subroutine for 1s
3. Move port 2 (P2) to the accumulator
4. Rotate right accumulator
5. Move the accumulator to port 2 (P2)
6. Jump to step 2

Program:

Assembly Language:

Label	Mnemonics & Operand(s)	Comments
	ORG 00H	Program starts from 0000H
	LJMP MAIN	Long jump to MAIN
	ORG 100H	Main source code starts from 100H
MAIN:	MOV P2, #0x80	Move 10000000 to PORT2
AGAIN:	CALL **Delay**	Call Delay Subroutine for 1 sec
	MOV A, P2	Move P2 to accumulator
	RR A	Rotate right accumulator
	MOV P2, A	Move accumulator to P2
	LJMP AGAIN	Jump to AGAIN
Delay:	MOV R1, #0x14	Move count value to **R1** **20** x 50 ms = 1000 ms = 1 sec
RPT:	MOV TH0, #0x3C	THO = 0x3C and TL0 = 0xAF
	MOV TL0, #0x0AF	
	MOV TMOD, #0x01	TMOD = 0x01
	SETB TR0	Start Timer0, TR0=1
Wait:	JNB TF0, **Wait**	Wait until the TF0 is set
	CLR TR0	Stop Timer0, TR0=0
	CLR TF0	Clear Timer0 flag, TF0=0

	DJNZ R1, **RPT**	Decrement count value (R1) and jump to RPT until R1=0
	RET	Return to main program
	END	End directive to suspend the program

Embedded C:

```
#include<reg51.h>              // include 8051 MCU header file
sfr output = 0xA0;            // Defining port 2 for LEDs

void delay1ms (unsigned int);   // Function declaration

void main (void)
{
   output = 0x80;               // P2 = 0x80
   while(1)                     // infinite loop
   {
     delay1ms (1000);          // Call delay function for 1 sec
     output = output >> 1;     // Right shift by 1 bit
        if (output == 0x00)    // Make rotation
        {
        output = 0x80;
        }
   }
}


// Timer0 mode 1- 1ms delay
void delay1ms (unsigned int t)
{
unsigned int i;
for(i=0;i<t; i++)
{
TH0=0xfc;                    // Timer register value for 1 ms
TL0=0x66;
TMOD=0x01;                   // Timer 0 – mode 1
TR0=1;                       // Start timer
while(TF0==0);               // Wait until TF0 is set
TR0=0;                       // Stop timer0
```

TF0=0;   // Clear Timer0 flag
}
}

Experimental Result – Circuit Diagram:

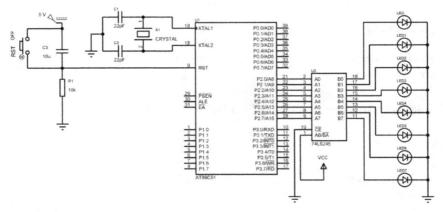

Conclusion:

The assembly language and embedded C programs for ring counter have been executed using the 8051 microcontroller.

2.16	KEY AND RELAY INTERFACE

Aim:

Write an 8051 assembly language and Embedded C programs for key and relay interface.

Apparatus:

o   8051 Microcontroller kit, Key and Electromagnetic relay

Software Required:

o   Keil μVision IDE / EdSim51DI Simulator/ any other supportive tool

Algorithm:

1. Clear the output port P2.0 to de-energies the relay
2. Wait for key press
3. Call delay subroutine
4. Complement the port P2.0
5. Wait for key de-bounce
6. Jump to step 2

Program:

Assembly Language:

Label	Mnemonics & Operand(s)	Comments
	ORG 00H	Program starts from 0000H
	Key EQU P1.0	Initialize P1.0 for Key
	Relay EQU P2.0	Initialize P2.0 for Relay
	LJMP MAIN	Long jump to MAIN
	ORG 100H	Main source code starts from 100H
MAIN:	CLR Relay	Clear P2.0
AGAIN:	JB Key, AGAIN	Jump to AGAIN if Key =1
	CALL Delay	Call delay subroutine
	CPL Relay	Complement Relay
STAY:	JNB Key, STAY	Jump to STAY if Key = 0
	LJMP AGAIN	Jump to AGAIN
Delay:	MOV R0, #0FFH	Move count value FFH to **R0**
Loop:	DJNZ R0, Loop	Decrement R0 and jump to Loop until R0 is zero
	RET	Return to main program
	END	End directive to suspend the program

Embedded C:

```
#include<reg51.h>              // include 8051 MCU header file
sbit Key = P1^0;               // Connect Key to P1.0
sbit Relay = P2^0;             // Connect Relay to P2.0
void delay1ms (unsigned int);  // Function declaration

void main (void)
{
    Relay = 0;                 // Clear P2.0
    while(1)                   // infinite loop
    {
        while (Key == 1);      // Wait for Key press
        delay1ms (1);          // Call delay function
        Relay = ~ Relay;       // Complement P2.0
        while (Key == 0);      // Wait for key de-bounce
    }
}


// Timer0 mode 1- 1ms delay
void delay1ms (unsigned int t) {
unsigned int i;
        for(i=0;i<t; i++)
        {
        TH0=0xfc;              // Timer register value for 1 ms
        TL0=0x66;
        TMOD=0x01;             // Timer 0 – mode 1
        TR0=1;                 // Start timer
        while(TF0==0);         // Wait until TF0 is set
        TR0=0;                 // Stop timer0
        TF0=0;                 // Clear Timer0 flag
        }
}
```

Experimental Result – Circuit Diagram:

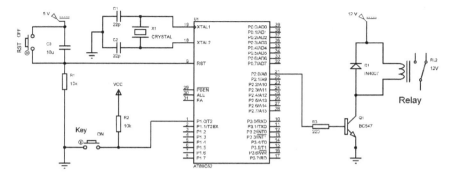

Conclusion:

The assembly language and embedded C programs for key and relay interface have been executed using the 8051 microcontroller.

2.17	SEVEN SEGMENT DISPLAY INTERFACE

Aim:

Write an 8051 assembly language and Embedded C programs for the seven-segment display interface.

Apparatus:

- o   8051 Microcontroller kit, Seven segment display (CA)

Software Required:

- o   Keil μVision IDE / EdSim51DI Simulator/ any other supportive tool

Algorithm:

1.   Clear the seven segment display
2.   Move count value to R0 for number of characters
3.   Initialize DPTR (500H) for seven segment codes
4.   Move the seven segment code to P2
5.   Call delay subroutine

6. Clear accumulator
7. Increment DPTR
8. Decrement R0 and jump to step 4 until R0 is zero
9. Jump to step 1

Seven Segment Display Code Generations in HEX for CA model:

Value		P2.7	P2.6	P2.5	P2.4	P2.3	P2.2	P2.1	P2.0
Digit	HEX	dp	g	f	e	d	c	b	a
0	0×C0	1	1	0	0	0	0	0	0
1	0×F9	1	1	1	1	1	0	0	1
2	0×A4	1	0	1	0	0	1	0	0
3	0×B0	1	0	1	1	0	0	0	0
4	0×99	1	0	0	1	1	0	0	1
5	0×92	1	0	0	1	0	0	1	0
6	0×83	1	0	0	0	0	0	1	1
7	0×F8	1	1	1	1	1	0	0	0
8	0×80	1	0	0	0	0	0	0	0
9	0×98	1	0	0	1	1	0	0	0
A	0x88	1	0	0	0	1	0	0	0
B	0x83	1	0	0	0	0	0	1	1
C	0xC3	1	1	0	0	0	0	1	1
D	0xA1	1	0	1	0	0	0	0	1
E	0x86	1	0	0	0	0	1	1	0
F	0x8E	1	0	0	0	1	1	1	0

Program:

Assembly Language:

Label	Mnemonics & Operand(s)	Comments
	ORG 00H	Program starts from 0000H

	LJMP **MAIN**	Long jump to MAIN
	ORG 500H DB 0xC0, 0xF9, 0xA4, 0xB0, 0x99, 0x92, 0x82, 0xF8, 0x80, 0x98, 0x88, 0x83, 0xc6, 0xa1, 0x86, 0x8e	
	ORG 100H	Main source code starts from 100H
MAIN:	MOV P2, #0FFH	Clear seven segment display
	MOV R0, #10H	Count for no of characters (0 to F)
	MOV DPTR, #500H	Move 500H to DPTR to points seven segment codes
NEXT:	MOVC A, @A+DPTR	Move the seven segment code to accumulator
	MOV P2, A	Move the accumulator to P2
	CALL Delay	Call delay subroutine for 1 sec
	CLR A	Clear accumulator
	INC DPTR	Increment DPTR
	DJNZ R0, **NEXT**	Decrement R0 and jump to NEXT until the R0 value is zero
	LJMP MAIN	Jump to MAIN
Delay:	MOV R1, #0x14	Move count value to **R1** **20** x 50 ms = 1000 ms = 1 sec
RPT:	MOV TH0, #0x3C	TH0 = 0x3C and TL0 = 0xAF
	MOV TL0, #0x0AF	
	MOV TMOD, #0x01	TMOD = 0x01
	SETB TR0	Start Timer0, TR0=1
Wait:	JNB TF0, **Wait**	Wait until the TF0 is set
	CLR TR0	Stop Timer0, TR0=0
	CLR TF0	Clear Timer0 flag, TF0=0
	DJNZ R1, **RPT**	Decrement count value (R1) and jump to RPT until R1=0

	RET	Return to main program
	END	End directive to suspend the program

Embedded C:

```
#include<reg51.h>              // include 8051 MCU header file
sfr segment = 0xA0;            // Defining port 2 for 7-segment

void delay1ms (unsigned int);   // Function declaration

void main (void)
{
unsigned int CA[] = {0xC0, 0xF9, 0xA4, 0xB0, 0x99, 0x92, 0x82, 0xF8,
0x80, 0x98, 0x88, 0x83, 0xc6, 0xa1, 0x86, 0x8e};
unsigned int i;
    while(1)                    // infinite loop
    {
        for (i=0; i<16; i++)
        {
        segment = CA[i];
        delay1ms (1000);
        }
    }
}


// Timer0 mode 1- 1ms delay
void delay1ms (unsigned int t)
{
unsigned int i;
for(i=0;i<t; i++)
{
TH0=0xfc;                  // Timer register value for 1 ms
TL0=0x66;
TMOD=0x01;                 // Timer 0 – mode 1
TR0=1;                     // Start timer
while(TF0==0);             // Wait until TF0 is set
TR0=0;                     // Stop timer0
TF0=0;                     // Clear Timer0 flag
```

}
}

Experimental Result – Circuit Diagram:

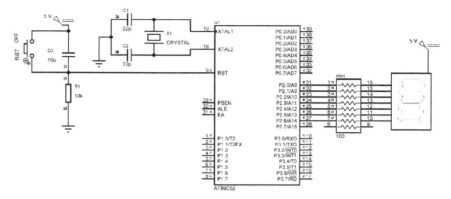

Conclusion:

The assembly language and embedded C programs for the seven-segment display interface have been executed using the 8051 microcontroller.

2.18 | SECONDS COUNTER USING 7-SEGMENT DISPLAY

Aim:

Write an 8051 Embedded C program for seconds counter using seven-segment displays.

Apparatus:

- o 8051 Microcontroller kit, 74LS373, Seven segment display (CA)

Software Required:

- o Keil μVision IDE / EdSim51DI Simulator/ any other supportive tool

Algorithm:

1. Initialize the variables i, j for LSB and MSB digits index
2. Enable the LSB digit
3. Move the seven-segment code to it
4. Enable the MSB digit
5. Move the seven-segment code to it
6. Call delay subroutine for 1 sec
7. Check LSB digit and clear if it is equal to 10, and increment MSB digit
8. Check MSB digit and clear if it is equal to 6
9. Jump to step 2

Seven Segment Display Code Generations in HEX for CA model:

Value		P2.7	P2.6	P2.5	P2.4	P2.3	P2.2	P2.1	P2.0
Digit	HEX	dp	g	f	e	d	c	b	a
0	0×C0	1	1	0	0	0	0	0	0
1	0×F9	1	1	1	1	1	0	0	1
2	0×A4	1	0	1	0	0	1	0	0
3	0×B0	1	0	1	1	0	0	0	0
4	0×99	1	0	0	1	1	0	0	1
5	0×92	1	0	0	1	0	0	1	0
6	0×83	1	0	0	0	0	0	1	1
7	0×F8	1	1	1	1	1	0	0	0
8	0×80	1	0	0	0	0	0	0	0
9	0×98	1	0	0	1	1	0	0	0

Program:
Embedded C:

```
// seconds count in seven segment displays using Timer0
#include<reg52.h>
sbit DIG1=P1^0;                    // P1.0 – Digit 1
```

```
sbit DIG2=P1^1;                 // P1.1 – Digit 2
sfr data1=0xA0;                 // P2.0-2.6 ==> segment bus (a to g)
void delay1ms (unsigned int);   // Function declaration
unsigned int value[10]={0xC0, 0xF9, 0xA4, 0xB0, 0x99, 0x92, 0x82, 0xF8,
0x80, 0x98};                    // 7-segment codes for CA

void main()
{
unsigned int i=0, j=0;          // j is LSB index and I is MSB index
        while(1)
        {
        DIG1=1;                 // Enable LSB digit
        DIG2=0;
        data1 = value[j];       // move the segment code to display
        DIG1=0;
        DIG2=1;                 // Enable MSB digit
        data1 = value[i];       // move the segment code to display
        delay1ms(1000);         // function calling for 1 sec
         j++;                   // increment seconds
                if (j==10)      // if LSB digit reach 10
                {
                j=0;            // clear LSB digit
                i++;            // increment MSB digit
                }
                if(i==6)        // if MSB digit reach 6
                {
                i=0;            // clear MSB digit
                }
        }
}

// Timer0 mode 1- 1ms delay
void delay1ms (unsigned int t)
{
```

```
unsigned int i;
for(i=0;i<t; i++)
{
THO=0xfc;               // Timer register value for 1 ms
TL0=0x66;
TMOD=0x01;              // Timer 0 – mode 1
TR0=1;                  // Start timer
while(TF0==0);          // Wait until TF0 is set
TR0=0;                  // Stop timer0
TF0=0;                  // Clear Timer0 flag
}
}
```

Experimental Result – Circuit Diagram:

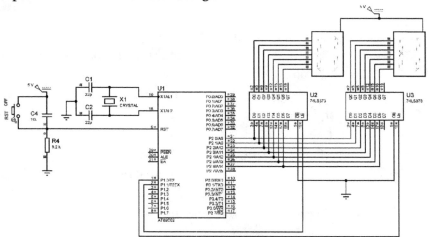

Conclusion:

The embedded C language program for the seconds counter has been executed using the 8051 microcontroller.

2.19	LCD DISPLAY INTERFACE

Aim:

Write an Embedded C program to interface 16x2 LCD with 8051 microcontroller and display the characters on LCD screen.

Apparatus:

o   8051 Microcontroller kit, 16x2 LCD

Software Required:

o   Keil µVision IDE / EdSim51DI Simulator/ any other supportive tool

Background:

16×2 LCD is an output device that will show any data or information to the user. The name 16×2 LCD means 16 numbers of data can be written on two lines. The data can be numbers (0-9) or letters (A-Z) or (a-z) or any symbol or space.

LCD Pin descriptions

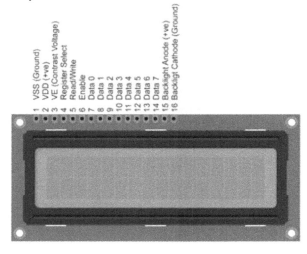

• **Vss/GND, Vdd, VE & +Ve**

- o Supply +5V to Vdd(pin2) and +Ve (pin15)
- o Connect Ground to Vss (pin1) and backlight cathode (pin16)
- o VE is used to control the contrast of the LCD screen.

- **RS, Register select**
  - o There are two important registers in the LCD. One is a data register and the other is the command register.
  - o If data is sent to data register the data is considered as data to be displayed on the LCD. If the command is sent to the command register which configures the LCD.
    * If RS=0, the command register is selected
    * If RS=1, the data register is selected

- **R/W, Read/Write**
  It is an input pin that allows the user to read data from the LCD or write data into the LCD.
  * To write data to LCD connect R/W pin to GND
  * To read data from LCD connect R/W pin to VCC

No.	Command	Hex value
1	Function Set: 8-bit, 1 Line, 5x7 Dots	0x30
2	Function Set: 8-bit, 2 Line, 5x7 Dots	0x38
3	Function Set: 4-bit, 1 Line, 5x7 Dots	0x20
4	Function Set: 4-bit, 2 Line, 5x7 Dots	0x28
5	Entry Mode	0x06
6	Display off Cursor off	0x08
7	Display on Cursor on	0x0E
8	Display on Cursor off	0x0C
9	Display on Cursor blinking	0x0F
10	Shift entire display left	0x18
11	Shift entire display right	0x1C
12	Move cursor left by one character	0x10
13	Move cursor right by one character	0x14

- **Enable (E)**
  - o Enable pin is used to latch the information on the data bus. A high to low pulse must be provided to enable pin.

- **D0 to D7**
  - ○ 8 data pins used to write command to LCD and read or write data to LCD.

Algorithm:

1. Initialize the char variable to display string "16x2 LCD Display" on screen
2. Send the basic command codes to LCD (0x38, 0x0E, 0x06)
3. Send the command to clear screen
4. Send the command to set the cursor on the first character in line 1
5. Send the string "16x2 LCD Display" to LCD
6. Call delay subroutine for 2 sec
7. Jump to step 3

Program:
Embedded C:

```
#include<reg52.h>
sfr lcd = 0xa0;              // port 2.0-2.7 ==> D0-D7 of LCD
sbit rs =P3^0;              // P3.0 = RS of LCD
sbit rw =P3^1;              // P3.1 = RW of LCD
sbit e =P3^2;               // P3.2 = E of LCD

void delay1ms (unsigned int);       // function declarations
void lcd_command(unsigned int);
void lcd_data(unsigned char);

void main()                 // main function
{
unsigned int k;
unsigned char a[]={"16x2 LCD Display"}; // Characters on display

lcd_command(0x38);          // Basic Commands to LCD
delay1ms (10);
lcd_command(0x0e);
delay1ms (10);
lcd_command(0x06);
delay1ms (10);
```

```
        while(1)
        {
        lcd_command(0x01);              // Clear LCD screen
        delay1ms (10);
        lcd_command(0x80);              // Command for line 1 first char
        delay1ms (10);

        for (k=0;k<16;k++)              // Displaying string on first line
        {
        lcd_data(a[k]);
        delay1ms (200);
        }
        delay1ms (2000);
        }
}
void delay1ms (unsigned int t)          // Timer0 mode 1- 1ms delay
{
unsigned int i;
for(i=0;i<t; i++)
{
TH0=0xfc;                               // Timer register value for 1 ms
TL0=0x66;
TMOD=0x01;                              // Timer 0 – mode 1
TR0=1;                                  // Start timer
while(TF0==0);                          // Wait until TF0 is set
TR0=0;                                  // Stop timer0
TF0=0;                                  // Clear Timer0 flag
}
}

void lcd_command(unsigned int c)        // Send command code to LCD
{
lcd=c;
rs=0;
rw=0;
e=1;                                    // High to Low pulse to EN pin
delay1ms (1);
e=0;
```

```
delay1ms (1);
}

void lcd_data(unsigned char d)        // Send data to LCD
{
lcd=d;
rs=1;
rw=0;
e=1;                                  // High to Low pulse to EN pin
delay1ms (1);
e=0;
delay1ms (1);
}
```

Experimental Result – Circuit Diagram:

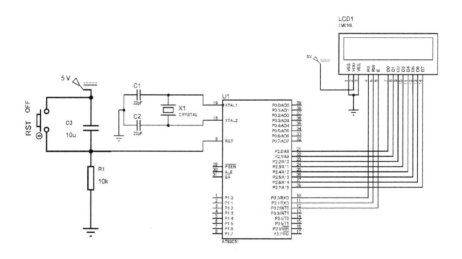

Conclusion:

The 16x2 LCD has been interfaced with the 8051 microcontroller and some characters have been displayed on the LCD screen.

2.20	HEX KEYBOARD INTERFACE

Aim:

Write an Embedded C program to interface Hex keyboard with 8051 microcontroller and display the pressed key character on the LCD screen.

Apparatus:

o 8051 Microcontroller kit, Hex key board, 16x2 LCD

Software Required:

o Keil μVision IDE / EdSim51DI Simulator/ any other supportive tool

Background:

Hex keyboard is a collection of 16 keys arranged in the form of a 4×4 matrix. Typically a hex keyboard has keys representing numbers 0, 1, 2, 3, 4, 5, 6, 7, 8, 9 and letters A, B, C, D, *, and #. The hex keyboard has 8 communication lines namely R1, R2, R3, R4 and C1, C2, C3 and C4 representing the rows and columns respectively. When a particular key is pressed the corresponding row and column to which the terminals of the key are connected (shorted). The diagram of a typical hex keypad is shown in the figure below.

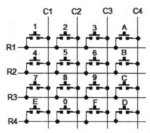

The column scanning method is used to identify the pressed key. In this method, a particular row is kept low whereas other rows are high. The logic status of each column line is scanned. If a particular column is found low, that means the key comes in between that column and row is short(pressed).

Algorithm:

1. Initialize port 3 for hex keyboard (LSB of port 3 representing column lines and MSB of port 3 representing row lines)
2. Initialize the port 1.0, port 1.1, port 1.2 and port 2 for 16x2 LCD
3. Configure the 16x2 LCD for 2 rows and 8-bit mode
4. Send the command to clear the screen and set the cursor at line1
5. Display the string " * Pressed Key * " on screen
6. Call the read_switch function and assign the return character to the 'key' variable
7. Set the cursor position to display the pressed key character on the second line of LCD
8. Jump to step 6

Algorithm for read_switch function:

1. Make R4 zero and other rows are high, scan columns to identify the LOW signal, if yes, return the pressed key character or if no, go to the next step.
2. Make R3 zero and other rows are high, scan columns to identify the LOW signal, if yes, return the pressed key character or if no, go to the next step.
3. Make R2 zero and other rows are high, scan columns to identify the LOW signal, if yes, return the pressed key character or if no, go to the next step.
4. Make R1 zero and other rows are high, scan columns to identify the LOW signal, if yes, return the pressed key character or if no, return the same character.

Program:
Embedded C:

```
#include<regx52.h>
sbit c1 = P3^0;                    // Ports assignment to Hex Keyboard
sbit c2 = P3^1;
sbit c3 = P3^2;
sbit c4 = P3^3;
```

```
sbit r1 = P3^4;
sbit r2 = P3^5;
sbit r3 = P3^6;
sbit r4 = P3^7;
sbit RS = P1^0;                          // Ports assignment to 16x2 LCD
sbit RW = P1^1;
sbit E = P1^2;
sfr data1 = 0xA0;


// 0      1      2      3               // Pattern of Hex key board
// 4      5      6      7
// 8      9      A      B
// C      D      E      F


void msdelay(unsigned int );     // Functions declaration
char read_switch(void);
void lcd_cmd(int);
void lcd_data(char);
void lcd_init(void);
char a[]={" * Pressed Key * "};  // Variable declaration and initialization
int i;
char key;


void main(void)                  // Main funciton
{
P1=0x00;                         // Clear ports
P2=0x00;
P3=0x0F;


lcd_init();                      // Function call to initialize the LCD
while(1)                         // forever loop
{
key = read_switch();             // Function call to read pressed key
lcd_cmd(0xC7);                   // bring cursor to position 8 of line 2
```

```
msdelay(10);
lcd_data(key);                    // display pressed key
}
}


char read_switch(void)            // Key read function
{
r4=0; r3=1; r2=1; r1=1; msdelay(10);        // Make R4=0 and scan columns
if (c4==0){msdelay(50); while(c4==0); return 'F';}
if (c3==0){msdelay(50); while(c3==0); return 'E';}
if (c2==0){msdelay(50); while(c2==0); return 'D';}
if (c1==0){msdelay(50); while(c1==0); return 'C';}

r4=1; r3=0; r2=1; r1=1; msdelay(10);        // Make R3=0 and scan columns
if (c4==0){msdelay(50); while(c4==0); return 'B';}
if (c3==0){msdelay(50); while(c3==0); return 'A';}
if (c2==0){msdelay(50); while(c2==0); return '9';}
if (c1==0){msdelay(50); while(c1==0); return '8';}

r4=1; r3=1; r2=0; r1=1; msdelay(10);        // Make R2=0 and scan columns
if (c4==0){msdelay(50); while(c4==0); return '7';}
if (c3==0){msdelay(50); while(c3==0); return '6';}
if (c2==0){msdelay(50); while(c2==0); return '5';}
if (c1==0){msdelay(50); while(c1==0); return '4';}

r4=1; r3=1; r2=1; r1=0; msdelay(10);        // Make R1=0 and scan columns
if (c4==0){msdelay(50); while(c4==0); return '3';}
if (c3==0){msdelay(50); while(c3==0); return '2';}
if (c2==0){msdelay(50); while(c2==0); return '1';}
if (c1==0){msdelay(50); while(c1==0); return '0';}
return (key);
}
void msdelay(unsigned int value)          // function for ms_delay
{
```

```
unsigned int i,j;
for(j=0;j<=value;j++)
for(i=0;i<=1275;i++);
}


void lcd_cmd(int x)        // function for sending command to LCD
{
data1=x;
RW=0;
RS=0;
E=1;
msdelay(5);
E=0;
msdelay(5);
}


void lcd_data(char y)     // function for sending data to LCD
{
data1=y;
RW=0;
RS=1;
E=1;
msdelay(5);
E=0;
msdelay(5);
}
void lcd_init(void)        // function to initialize LCD
{
lcd_cmd(0x38);             // for 8-bit, 2 rows mode
msdelay(10);
lcd_cmd(0x0C);             // turn display ON for cursor off
msdelay(10);
lcd_cmd(0x01);             //clear screen
msdelay(10);
```

```
lcd_cmd(0x06);          //Entry mode
msdelay(10);
lcd_cmd(0x80);          // bring cursor to position 1 of line 1
msdelay(10);
for (i=0;i<16;i++)      // Display "* Pressed Key * "
{
lcd_data(a[i]);
msdelay(10);
}
}
```

Experimental Result – Circuit Diagram:

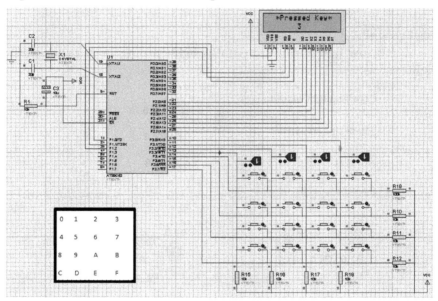

Conclusion:

The hex key board has been interfaced with the 8051 microcontroller and the pressed key character is displayed on the LCD screen.

2.21	TRAFFIC LIGHT CONTROLLER

Aim:

Write an Embedded C program for the traffic light controller using the 8051 microcontroller.

Apparatus:

o   8051 Microcontroller kit, Traffic light module

Software Required:

o   Keil μVision IDE / EdSim51DI Simulator/ any other supportive tool

Background:

The below figure shows the traffic lights arrangement of the traffic light system.

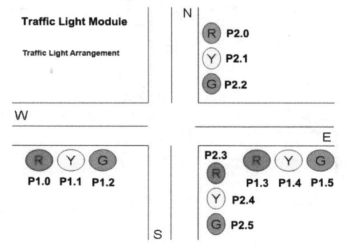

The traffic light sequence for the traffic light controller is described as follows,

1) Allow traffic from W to E and E to W transition for 10 seconds.

2) Give transition time of 2 seconds (Yellow bulbs ON)

3) Allow traffic from N to Sand S to N for 10 seconds

4) Give transition time of 2 seconds (Yellow bulbs ON)

5) Repeat the process.

Traffic light sequence and its equivalent Hex code:

South			North			East			West			HEX
Green	Yellow	Red	Green	Yellow	Red	Green	Yellow	Red	Green	Yellow	Red	P2/P1
P2.5	P2.4	P2.3	P2.2	P2.1	P2.0	P1.5	P1.4	P1.3	P1.2	P1.1	P1.0	
0	0	1	0	0	1	1	0	0	1	0	0	09/24
Delay for 10 seconds												
0	1	0	0	1	0	0	1	0	0	1	0	12/12
Delay for 2 seconds												
1	0	0	1	0	0	0	0	1	0	0	1	24/09
Delay for 10 seconds												
0	1	0	0	1	0	0	1	0	0	1	0	12/12
Delay for 2 seconds												

Algorithm:

1. Clear port 2 and port 1
2. Send the data 09H and 24H to port 2 and port 1 respectively
3. Call delay subroutine for 10 seconds
4. Send the data 12H and 12H to port 2 and port 1 respectively
5. Call delay subroutine for 2 seconds
6. Send the data 24H and 09H to port 2 and port 1 respectively
7. Call delay subroutine for 10 seconds
8. Send the data 12H and 12H to port 2 and port 1 respectively
9. Call delay subroutine for 2 seconds
10. Jump to step 1

Program:
Embedded C:

```
#include<regx52.h>
sbit WR = P1^0;          // Ports assignment to West traffic lights
sbit WY = P1^1;
sbit WG = P1^2;
sbit ER = P1^3;          // Ports assignment to East traffic lights
sbit EY = P1^4;
sbit EG = P1^5;
sbit NR = P2^0;          // Ports assignment to North traffic lights
sbit NY = P2^1;
sbit NG = P2^2;
sbit SR = P2^3;          // Ports assignment to South traffic lights
sbit SY = P2^4;
sbit SG = P2^5;

void main ()
{
P1=0x0;                  // Clear Ports to turn-off all lights
P2=0x0;
        while (1)
        {
        P1= 0x24;        // Send traffic sequence code for step1
        P2= 0x09;
        delay1ms (10000);
        P1= 0x12;        // Send traffic sequence code for step2
        P2= 0x12;
        delay1ms (2000);
        P1= 0x09;        // Send traffic sequence code for step 3
        P2= 0x24;
        delay1ms (10000);
        P1= 0x12;        // Send traffic sequence code for step 4
        P2= 0x12;
        delay1ms (2000);
        }
}

void delay1ms (unsigned int t)          // Timer0 mode 1- 1ms delay
{
```

```
unsigned int i;
    for(i=0;i<t; i++)
    {
    TH0=0xfc;                          // Timer register value for 1 ms
    TL0=0x66;
    TMOD=0x01;                         // Timer 0 – mode 1
    TR0=1;                             // Start timer
    while(TF0==0);                     // Wait until TF0 is set
    TR0=0;                             // Stop timer0
    TF0=0;                             // Clear Timer0 flag
    }
}
```

Experimental Result – Circuit Diagram:

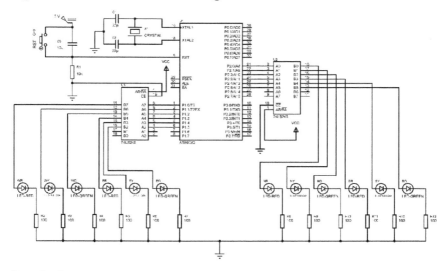

Conclusion:

The traffic light controller program has been executed using the 8051 microcontroller.

2.22	SOLID STATE RELAY INTERFACE

Aim:

Write an Embedded C program to interface solid state relay with the 8051 microcontroller and flash an AC lamp on and off.

Apparatus:

- o 8051 Microcontroller kit, Opto-coupler MOC3021, BC547, BT136, AC Lamp

Software Required:

- o Keil μVision IDE / EdSim51DI Simulator/ any other supportive tool

Background:

Solid-State Switches (SSS) are an electronic component that switches Power (AC or DC current) to a load and provides electrical isolation between an application control circuit and load.

It switches on or off when a small external voltage is applied across its control terminals.

It works based on an optocoupler principle, the device that transfers electrical signals between two electrically isolated circuits through light energy.

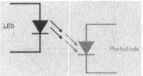

SSS has usually a Light Emitting Diode (LED) and a photo-thyristor that acting as the photo-sensor. It provides galvanic isolation between the input control circuit and the load.

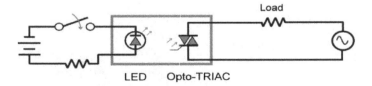

LED   Opto-TRIAC

Algorithm:

1. Initialize P2.0 for solid-state relay and P2.1 for LED
2. Turn-on the relay and LED
3. Call delay subroutine for 1 second
4. Turn-off the relay and LED
5. Call delay subroutine for 1 second
6. Jump to step 2

Program:

Embedded C:

```
#include<regx52.h>
sbit relay = P2^0;              // initialize P2.0 for solid state relay
sbit led = P2^1;               // initialize P2.1 for an LED

void delay1ms (unsigned int);  // function declaration

void main()                    // main function
{
        while(1)               // forever loop
        {
        relay=1;               // turn-on relay and LED
        led = 1;
        delay1ms (1000);       // call delay subroutine for 1 sec
        relay=0;               // turn-off relay and LED
        led=0;
        delay1ms (1000);       // call delay subroutine for 1 sec
        }
}

void delay1ms (unsigned int t)          // Timer0 mode 1- 1ms delay
{
unsigned int i;
        for(i=0;i<t; i++)
        {
        TH0=0xfc;                       // Timer register value for 1 ms
        TL0=0x66;
        TMOD=0x01;                      // Timer 0 – mode 1
        TR0=1;                          // Start timer
```

```
    while(TF0==0);          // Wait until TF0 is set
    TR0=0;                  // Stop timer0
    TF0=0;                  // Clear Timer0 flag
    }
}
```

Experimental Result – Circuit Diagram:

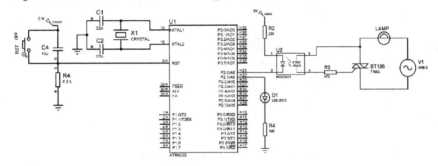

Conclusion:

The circuit for solid state relay interface has been constructed and the AC lamp has flashed using the 8051 microcontroller.

2.23	DC MOTOR DIRECTION CONTROLLER

Aim:

Write an Embedded C program to interface DC motor with the 8051 microcontroller and control its direction of rotation.

Apparatus:

o 8051 Microcontroller kit, NPN Transistors, Diodes, 6V DC motor

Software Required:

o Keil µVision IDE / EdSim51DI Simulator/ any other supportive tool

Algorithm:

1. Initialize P2.0 and P2.1 for H-bridge control

2. Initialize P1.0 and P1.1 for direction control inputs to MCU
3. Rotate motor clockwise direction if FRD = 0
4. Call delay subroutine for 2 second
5. Rotate motor anti-clockwise direction if REV = 0
6. Call delay subroutine for 2 second
7. Stop the motor rotation if FRD = 0 and REV = 0
8. Call delay subroutine for 2 second
9. Continues the motor rotation in last state if FRD = 1 and REV = 1
10. Call delay subroutine for 2 second
11. Jump to step 3

Program:
Embedded C:

```
#include<regx52.h>
sbit FRD = P1^0;          // Initialize P1.0 and P1.1 for direction control inputs
sbit REV = P1^1;          // Initialize P2.0 and P2.1 for H-bridge control
sbit motor_pin1 = P2^0;
sbit motor_pin2 = P2^1;
void delay1ms(unsigned int);
void main()                              // main function
{
while(1)
{
        if (FRD==0)
        {
        motor_pin1 = 0;                  //Rotates Motor Clockwise
        motor_pin2 = 1;
        delay1ms(2000);
        }
        if (REV==0)
        {
        motor_pin1 = 1;                  //Rotates Motor Anit Clockwise
        motor_pin2 = 0;
        delay1ms(2000);
```

```
        }
        if (FRD==0 && REV==0)              // Stop the rotation
        {
        motor_pin1 = 0;
        motor_pin2 = 0;
        delay1ms(2000);
        }
        if (FRD==1 && REV==1)              //No change in direction
        {
        motor_pin1 = motor_pin1;
        motor_pin2 = motor_pin2;
        delay1ms(2000);
        }
    }
}


void delay1ms (unsigned int t)            // Timer0 mode 1- 1ms delay
{
unsigned int i;
for(i=0;i<t; i++)
{
TH0=0xfc;                                 // Timer register value for 1 ms
TL0=0x66;
TMOD=0x01;                                // Timer 0 – mode 1
TR0=1;                                    // Start timer
while(TF0==0);                            // Wait until TF0 is set
TR0=0;                                    // Stop timer0
TF0=0;                                    // Clear Timer0 flag
}
}
```

Experimental Result – Circuit Diagram:

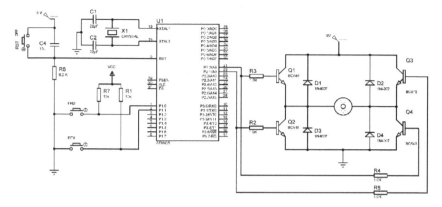

Conclusion:

The direction of rotation of a DC motor has been controlled using the 8051 microcontroller and H-bridge circuit.

2.24	OBJECT COUNTER USING INTERRUPT

Aim:

Write an Embedded C program for object counter using the external interrupt of 8051 microcontroller and display the count value on LCD.

Apparatus:

  o   8051 Microcontroller kit, Proximity sensor and 16x2 LCD

Software Required:

  o   Keil μVision IDE / EdSim51DI Simulator/ any other supportive tool

Algorithm:

1. Initialize P3.2 for proximity sensor
2. Initialize P2 and P1.0, P1.1, P1.2 for LCD

3. Configure LCD in 8-bit and 2 lines mode
4. Enable INT0 interrupt and global interrupt. (IE=0x81)
5. Make INT0 edge-sensitive (IT0=1)
6. Display the count value on LCD
7. Jump to step 6

ISR:
1. Increment the count value

Program:

Embedded C:

```
#include<regx52.h>
sbit obj = P3^2;            // proximity sensor input
sfr lcd = 0xA0;            // port 2 is connected with data bus of LCD
sbit rs = P1^0;            // control pins of LCD to P1.0, P1.1, P1.2
sbit rw = P1^1;
sbit e = P1^2;
void ms (unsigned int);            // function declarations
void lcd_command(unsigned int);
void lcd_data(unsigned char);
void lcd_init();
int count,d,d1,d2,d3;


void main()                // main function
{
        lcd_init();                // Initialize LCD
        IE = 0x81;                 // Enable /INT0 and global interrupts
        IT0 = 1;                   // Make INT0 edge sensitive
        count=0;
        while(1)
        {
        d = count;
        d1=(d/100)+48;             // Digit extraction & ASCII conversion
        d2=((d%100)/10)+48;
        d3=(d%10)+48;
```

```
        lcd_command(0xc6);    // display the count value
        ms (5);
        lcd_data(d1);
        ms (5);
        lcd_data(d2);
        ms (5);
        lcd_data(d3);
        ms (5);
        }
}


// Subroutines
void ex0_isr (void) interrupt 0   // ISR
{
count++;                          // increment the count value
}

void ms (unsigned int t)          // Timer0 mode 1- 1ms delay
{
unsigned int i;
for(i=0;i<t; i++)
{
TH0=0xfc;                         // Timer register value for 1 ms
TL0=0x66;
TMOD=0x01;                        // Timer 0 – mode 1
TR0=1;                            // Start timer
while(TF0==0);                    // Wait until TF0 is set
TR0=0;                            // Stop timer0
TF0=0;                            // Clear Timer0 flag
}
}

void lcd_command(unsigned int c)      // LCD command write function
{
lcd=c;
rs=0;
```

```
rw=0;
e=1;
ms(1);
e=0;
ms(1);
}

void lcd_data(unsigned char d)          // LCD data write function
{
lcd=d;
rs=1;
rw=0;
e=1;
ms(1);
e=0;
ms(1);
}


void lcd_init()                          // LCD initialization
{
unsigned int k;
unsigned char a[]={" No. of Objects "};
lcd_command(0x38);
ms (5);
lcd_command(0x0e);
ms (5);
lcd_command(0x01);
ms (5);
lcd_command(0x06);
ms (5);
lcd_command(0x80);
ms (5);
for (k=0;k<16;k++)
{
lcd_data(a[k]);
ms (50);
}
}
```

Experimental Result – Circuit Diagram:

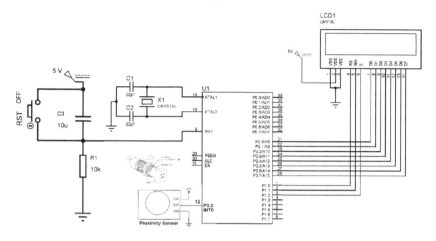

Conclusion:

The objection counter has been designed and performed using the 8051 microcontroller.

| 2.25 | INTERFACING 8-BIT DAC |

Aim:

Write Embedded C programs for interfacing DAC with the 8051 microcontroller and generate the waveforms.

Apparatus:

o   8051 Microcontroller kit, DAC0800 and IC741

Software Required:

o   Keil μVision IDE / EdSim51DI Simulator/ any other supportive tool

Algorithm:

DAC0800 series are monolithic 8-bit high-speed current output digital-to-analog converters (DAC). Its typical settling time is 100 ns. The number of data bit inputs decides the resolution of the DAC. The digital inputs are converted to current output (I_{out}), and by connecting a pull-up resistor to the I_{out} pin for voltage output.

$$I_{out} = I_{ref} \left(\frac{D7}{2} + \frac{D6}{4} + \frac{D5}{8} + \frac{D4}{16} + \frac{D3}{32} + \frac{D2}{64} + \frac{D1}{128} + \frac{D0}{256} \right)$$

Square Wave Generation (1K Hz)

1. Move 00H to the Port 2
2. Call delay subroutine for 1 msec
3. Move FFH to Port 2
4. Call delay subroutine for 1 msec
5. Jump to step 1

Embedded C Program:

```
#include<regx52.h>
sfr DAC = 0xA0;                    //Port P2 address
void delay1ms (unsigned int);      // function declaration

void main()                        // main function
{
while (1)
{
DAC = 0x00;                        // Move 00H to the P2
delay1ms (1);                      // call delay subroutine
DAC = 0xFF;                        // Move FFH to the P2
delay1ms (1);                      // call delay subroutine
}
}

void delay1ms (unsigned int t)     // Timer0 mode 1- 1ms delay
{
unsigned int i;
for(i=0;i<t; i++)
```

```
{
TH0=0xfc;                    // Timer register value for 1 ms
TL0=0x66;
TMOD=0x01;                   // Timer 0 – mode 1
TR0=1;                       // Start timer
while(TF0==0);               // Wait until TF0 is set
TR0=0;                       // Stop timer0
TF0=0;                       // Clear Timer0 flag
}
}
```

Sawtooth Wave Generation

1. Clear Port 2
2. Increment Port 2
3. Call small delay (100 ns) to recover DAC
4. Jump to step 2

Embedded C Program:

```
#include<regx52.h>
sfr DAC = 0xA0;              //Port P2 address

void main()                  // main function
{
unsigned int i;
DAC = 0x00;                  // clear P2
while (1)                    // forever loop
{
DAC = DAC + 1;               // Increment P2
for (i=0; i<200; i++);       // small delay
}
}
```

Triangular Wave Generation

1. Clear accumulator
2. Move accumulator to the Port 2
3. Increment the accumulator
4. Call small delay (100 ns) to recover DAC
5. Compare accumulator with FFH if it is not equal jump to step 2
6. Move accumulator to the Port 2
7. Decrement the accumulator
8. Call small delay (100 ns) to recover DAC
9. Compare accumulator with 00H if it is not equal jump to step 6
10. Jump to step 1

Embedded C Program:

```
#include<regx52.h>
sfr DAC = 0xA0;                    //Port P2 address
void main()                        // main function
{
unsigned int i, k;
        while (1)                  // forever loop
        {
        DAC = 0x00;                // clear P2
        for (k=0; k<250;k++)       // Increment P2 for 250 times
        {
        DAC = DAC + 1;
        for (i=0; i<200; i++);
        }

        for (k=250; k>0; k--)      // Decrement P2 for 250 times
        {
        DAC = DAC - 1;
        for (i=0; i<200; i++);
        }
        }
}
```

Sine Wave Generation

The values for the sine function vary from -1.0 to +1.0 for 0 to 360-degree angles. The look-up table values are representing the voltage magnitude for the sine of theta. Let us take 10 V as the full-scale voltage for DAC output. Therefore, the output voltage is,

$$V_{out} = 5v + (5 * \sin \theta)$$

1. Initialize the sine wave values (16 nos) in an integer array.
2. Create for loop with target value 16.
3. Move the sine wave value to Port 2 and repeat step 3 until the suspension of for loop.
4. Jump to step 2.

Embedded C Program:

```
#include<regx52.h>
sfr DAC = 0xA0;                        //Port P2 address
void main()
{
int sin_value [16]={127, 176, 218, 245, 255, 245, 218, 176, 128, 79, 37, 10, 0,
10, 37, 79};
int i;
        while(1)                        //infinite loop
        {
        for (i = 0; i<16; i++)          // for loop for 16
        {
                DAC = sin_value[i];     // move sine value to P2
        }
        }
}
```

Experimental Result – Circuit Diagram:

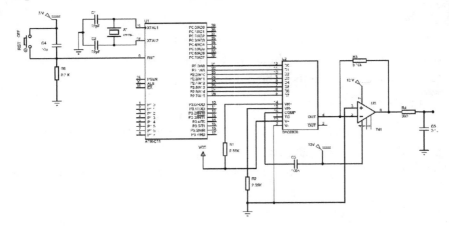

Conclusion:

The DAC0800 has been interfaced with the 8051 microcontroller, and square waveform, sawtooth waveform, triangular waveform and sine waveform were generated.

2.26	INTERFACING 8-BIT ADC

Aim:

Write an Embedded C program to convert the analog value into an 8-bit digital value using ADC0804 and 8051 microcontroller.

Apparatus:

    o   8051 Microcontroller kit, ADC0804 and LEDs

Software Required:

    o   Keil µVision IDE / EdSim51DI Simulator/ any other supportive tool

Algorithm:

1. Initialize Port 2 for data bus D0-D7 of ADC
2. Initialize Port 1 for output LEDs

3. Initialize Port 3.0, P3.1, P3.2, P3.3 for chip select, RD, WR, and EOC signals respectively
4. Clear Port 1 (Turn-off output LEDs)
5. Make chip select active and disable read function
6. Raise the Start of Conversion (SOC) pulse through WR
7. Wait for EOC signal from ADC
8. Make read signal active
9. Read the data bus and move the data to Port 1 (LEDs)
10. Jump to step 5

Program:
Embedded C:

```
#include<regx52.h>

sfr data1 = 0xA0;        // Port 2 is connected with D0-D7 of ADC
sfr led = 0x90;          // Port 1 is connected with LEDs

sbit cs1 = P3^0;         // chip select (active low)
sbit rd1 = P3^1;         // RD signal (active low)
sbit wr1 = P3^2;         // WR signal
sbit eoc1 = P3^3;        // EOC signal (active low)

void delay (unsigned int x)     // Delay subroutine
{
unsigned int i,j;
for (i=0; i<x; i++)
{
for (j=0; j<123; j++);
}
}

void main()                     // main function
{
led = 0x00;                     // Clear Port 1 (Turn-off LEDs)
        while(1)
        {
                cs1 = 0;        // Enable the chip
                rd1 = 1;        // Disable read function
```

```
        delay(1);
        wr1 = 0;                    // SOC pulse
        delay(2);
        wr1 = 1;
        delay(2);

        while(eoc1 == 1);           // wait for EOC

        cs1 = 0;
        rd1 = 0;                    // RD signal active
        delay(2);
        led = data1;                // Move the ADC data to led
        delay(300);
    }
}
```

Experimental Result – Circuit Diagram:

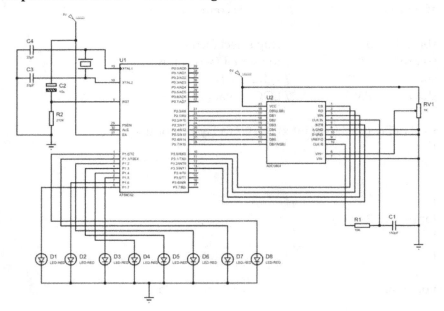

Conclusion:

The ADC0804 has been interfaced with the 8051 microcontroller and the digital values are indicated on LEDs to the analog inputs.

2.27	STEPPER MOTOR INTERFACE

Aim:

Write an embedded C program to interface stepper motor with the 8051 microcontroller and rotate for 360 degree clock wise and 360 degree anti-clockwise direction.

Apparatus:

- o 8051 Microcontroller kit, ULN 2003 motor driver and Stepper motor.

Software Required:

- o Keil μVision IDE / EdSim51DI Simulator/ any other supportive tool

Background:

Stepper motor is a brushless, synchronous DC electric motor, which divides the full rotation into a number of equal steps. It is also known as Step Motor. For example, in the case of a 200 step motor, one complete rotation (360°) is divided into 200 steps, which means one step is equal to 1.8°.

There are two types of stepper motors: Unipolar and Bipolar. Due to the ease of operation unipolar stepper motor is most widely used. A unipolar motor contains center-tapped windings. The center connection of the coils is tied together and used as the power terminal.

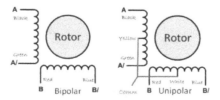

A standard motor will have the step angle of 1.8 degrees, then the number of steps required to complete one revolution will be

$$\text{Steps per Revolution} = 360^0 / \text{Step Angle}$$

$$= 360^0/1.8^0 = 200$$

Stepper motors can be driven in three different patterns or sequences. Namely,

Wave Step sequence: The motor is operated with only one phase energized at a time. It is the 4 step sequence.

Full Step Sequence: The motor is operated with two phases energized at a time. It is the 4 step sequence.

Half Step Sequence: In this method, coils are energized alternatively. Thus it rotates with half step angle. It is the 8 step sequence.

In Full Step Drive method, two coils are energized at a time. Thus, here two adjacent coils are excited at a time. It is the 4 step sequence.

Step	A	B	A/	B/	Hex Value
1	1	1	0	0	0x0C
2	0	1	1	0	0x06
3	0	0	1	1	0x03
4	1	0	0	1	0x09

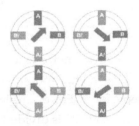

Stepper motor Connector:

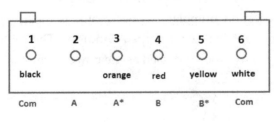

Algorithm:

1. Initialize Port 1 for the stepper motor driver
2. Declare the variables and initialize the full step sequence for clockwise and counter clockwise rotation
3. Use for loop to send 200 steps to the motor driver for 360 degrees

clock-wise rotation

4. Wait for 2 seconds
5. Use for loop to send 200 steps to the motor driver for 360 degrees counter clock-wise rotation
6. Wait for 2 seconds
7. Stop the program execution

Program:
Embedded C:

```
#include<regx52.h>
sfr step=0x90;                          // P1 is connected to driver
void delay1ms (unsigned int);

void main()
{
unsigned int i,j;
int ccw[]={0x0C,0x06,0x03,0x09};
int cw[]={0x09,0x03,0x06,0x0C};

// for 360 clk-wise rotation, 360/1.8 = 200 steps to send
        for (i=0; i<50; i++)
        {
        for(j=0; j<4; j++)
        {
        step=ccw[j];
        delay1ms (15);
        }
        }
delay1ms (2000);
// for 360 Anti-clk-wise rotation, 360/1.8 = 200 steps to send
        for (i=0; i<50; i++)
        {
        for(j=0; j<4; j++)
        {
        step=cw[j];
        delay1ms (15);
        }
        }
```

```
delay1ms (2000);
while(1);
}
void delay1ms (unsigned int t)              // Timer0 mode 1- 1ms delay
{
unsigned int i;
for(i=0;i<t; i++) {
TH0=0xfc;                                   // Timer register value for 1 ms
TL0=0x66;
TMOD=0x01;                                  // Timer 0 – mode 1
TR0=1;                                      // Start timer
while(TF0==0);                              // Wait until TF0 is set
TR0=0;                                      // Stop timer0
TF0=0;                                      // Clear Timer0 flag
}
}
```

Experimental Result – Circuit Diagram:

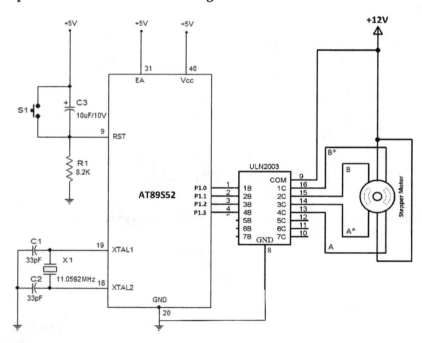

Conclusion:

The stepper motor has been interfaced with the 8051 microcontroller and the rotation of angle is controlled using step sequence.

2.28	SERIAL DATA COMMUNICATION

Aim:

Write an assembly language and embedded C program to control the LED through computer keyboard using the 8051 serial communication.

Apparatus:

- o 8051 Microcontroller kit, MAX 232 converter, RS232 Serial port cable and LED with resistor.

Software Required:

- o Keil μVision IDE / EdSim51DI Simulator/ any other supportive tool

Background:

8051 chip has a built-in UART. The 8051 serial port supports full-duplex communication and it can transmit and receive data at the same time. In asynchronous communication, at least two extra bits are transmitted with the data byte; a start bit and a stop bit. Each data (character) is placed between the start and stop bits is called data framing. The start bit is logic 0 while the stop bit is logic 1.

LSB is sent out first. Sometimes a parity bit is added along with the data as a 9th bit.

The number of bits transmitted or received per second (bps) is called baud rate. Baud rate should be the same in both transmitter and receiver.

Recommended Standard 232:

RS232 is set by the Electronics Industries Association (EIA) in 1962. It is the most widely used serial I/O interfacing standard. Input and output voltage levels are not TTL compatible

- Logic 0 -> +3 to +25 V
- Logic 1 -> -3 to -25 V
- -3 to +3 is undefined

To connect RS232 to a microcontroller system must use voltage converter such as MAX232 for converting the TTL logic to the RS232 logic, and vice versa. MAX232 IC chip is commonly referred to as line drivers.

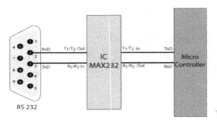

RxD and TxD pins in the 8051:

8051 has two pins used for transmitting and receiving data serially. TxD and RxD are part of the Port 3 group, these pins are TTL compatible. It requires a line driver to make them RS232 compatible

- Pin 10 (P3.0) is assigned to RxD
- Pin 11 (P3.1) is assigned to TxD

SCON (Serial Control Register) is responsible for all serial communication-related settings in 8051.

SBUF (Serial Buffer Register) is an 8-bit register used for serial communication.

- During transmission, a byte to be transmitted via the TxD line must be placed in the SBUF register.
- During the reception, SBUF receives the byte of data from receive line RxD.

Baud Rate Calculation:

If the external clock frequency is 11.0592 MHz, it is divided by 12 to get machine cycle frequency - 921.6 kHz.

8051's UART circuitry divides the machine cycle frequency of 921.6 kHz by 32.

Therefore, 921.6 kHz divided by 32 gives out 28,800 Hz.

- 28,800/3 = 9600 baud rate. Therefore -3 is loaded in TH1 (FDH)
- 28,800/6 = 4800 baud rate. Therefore -6 is loaded in TH1 (FAH)

Algorithm:

1. The TMOD register is loaded with the value 20H, indicating the use of Timer 1 in mode 2 (8-bit auto-reload) to set the baud rate
2. TH1 is loaded by FDH to set the baud rate 9600 for serial data transfer (assuming XTAL = 11.0592 MHz)
3. The SCON register is loaded with the value 50H, indicating serial mode 1, where 8-bit data is framed with start and stop bits and receive enable is turned on
4. TR1 is set to 1 to start Timer 1
5. RI is cleared
6. RI flag bit is monitored for the serial character
7. When RI is raised, SBUF has the received byte. It is tested whether Y or N for LED on/off
8. Then the received character is transmitted to PC

Program:

Assembly Language:

Label	Mnemonics & Operand(s)	Comments
	ORG 0000H	
AGAIN:	MOV TMOD, #20H	Timer1, mode 2 (Auto-reload)
	MOV TH1, #0FDH	9600 baud rate
	MOV SCON, #50H	8-bit data, 1 stop bit, REN enabled
	SETB TR1	Start timer1
	CLR RI	Clear serial receive interrupt flag
wait_rx:	JNB RI, **wait_rx**	Wait for character

	CLR RI	Clear serial receive interrupt flag
	CLR TR1	Stop timer1
	MOV A, SBUF	Move SBUF value to accumulator
	LCALL LED	Call LED subroutine
	CLR TI	Clear serial transmit interrupt flag
	SETB TR1	Start timer1
	MOV SBUF, A	Move accumulator to SBUF
wait_tx:	JNB TI, **wait_tx**	Wait for transmitting a character
	CLR TI	Clear serial transmit interrupt flag
	LJMP **AGAIN**	Jump to AGAIN
LED:	CJNE A, #'Y', **NEXT**	Test the received character is 'Y'. If not equal, jump to NEXT
	SETB P1.7	Turn-on LED at P1.7
	RET	Return to the main program
NEXT:	CJNE A, #'N', **NOC**	Test the received character is 'N'. If not equal, jump to **NOC**
	CLR P1.7	Turn-off LED at P1.7
NOC:	RET	Return to the main program
	END	End directive

Embedded C:

```
#include<regx52.h>
sbit LED = P1^7;            // Assign P1.7 for LED
void led_cnt();             // function declaration
unsigned int A;             // global variable declaration

void main ()                // main function
{
```

```
        while (1)                    // forever loop
        {
        TMOD = 0x20;                 // Timer1, mode 2 (Auto-reload)
        TH1 = 0xFD;                  // 9600 baud rate
        SCON = 0x50;                 // 8-bit data, 1 stop bit, REN enabled
        TR1 = 1;                     // start timer 1
        RI = 0;                      // clear serial receive interrupt flag
        while (RI == 0);             // wait for a character through RxD
        RI = 0;                      // clear serial receive interrupt flag
        TR1 = 0;                     // stop timer 1
        A = SBUF;                    // move SBUF to variable A
        led_cnt ();                  // call led_cnt() funcation
        TI = 0;                      // clear serial transmit interrupt flag
        TR1 = 1;                     // start timer 1
        SBUF = A;                    // load SBUF – character to be send
        while (TI == 0);             // wait for transmitting
        TI = 0;                      // clear serial transmit interrupt flag
        TR1 = 0;                     // stop timer 1
        }
}


void led_cnt() {                     // subroutine for LED control
        if ( A == 'Y')               // if character 'Y' received
        {
        LED = 1;                     // Turn-on LED
        }
        else if ( A == 'N')          // if character 'N' received
        {
        LED = 0;                     // Turn-off LED
        }
}
```

Experimental Result – Circuit Diagram:

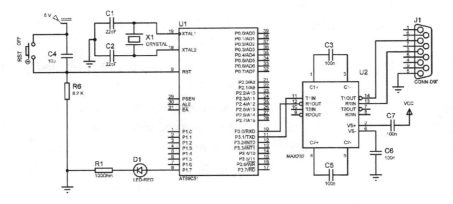

Conclusion:

The LED is controlled by keyboard from PC through RS232 using UART of 8051 microcontroller.

2.29	PWM BASED DC MOTOR SPEED CONTROL

Aim:

Write an Embedded C program for PWM based speed control of DC motor using the 8051 microcontroller.

Apparatus:

o 8051 Microcontroller kit and L298N motor driver module

Software Required:

o Keil μVision IDE / EdSim51DI Simulator/ any other supportive tool

Algorithm:

1. Initialize Port 2.0 and P2.1 for PWM duty cycle control
2. Initialize Port 2.2 for PWM output off
3. Initialize Port 1.7 for PWM output
4. Initialize the PWM duty cycle as 50%

5. Set all input ports to high
6. Clear PWM output
7. Initialize the timer 0 of 8051 for PWM signal generation
8. If DD key is zero, decrease the PWM duty cycle value by 10 for every press. Make sure the minimum duty cycle value is not less than 20
9. If ID key is zero, increase the PWM duty cycle value by 10 for every press. Make sure the maximum duty cycle value is not more than 240
10. If the stop key is pressed, PWM signal output is off
11. Repeat from step 8

Timer 0 ISR:
1. Stop timer 0
2. If PWM output is on, turn-off the PWM output and update the PWM duty cycle value
3. If PWM output is off, turn-on the PWM output and update the duty cycle value
4. Clear timer 0 flag
5. Run timer 0

Program:
Embedded C:

```
#include<regx51.h>
sbit DD = P2^0;                    // Port 2.0 and 2.1 are used
sbit ID = P2^1;                    // for Duty Cycle adjustment
sbit stop = P2^2;                  // P2.2 used to stop PWM out
sbit PWM_Out = P1^7;               // P1.7 is PWM output pin
void PWM_timer_Init (void);        // function declaration

unsigned char PWM1 = 125;          // 50% DD
unsigned int t = 0;
unsigned char x=1;
```

187

```c
void main(void)                       // Main function
{
        DD = ID = stop =1;            // set as '1'
        PWM_Out = 0;                  // Clear PWM output
        PWM_timer_Init ();            // function calling timer int
    while (1)                         // forever loop
    {
                if(DD==0)             // If DD key is pressed
                {
                PWM1 = PWM1-10;       // Decrease Duty cycle
                x=0;
                if (PWM1 <= 20)       // Setting Min DC as 20
                {
                PWM1=20;
                }
                }
                else if (ID==0)       // If ID key is pressed
                {
                PWM1 = PWM1+10;       // Increase Duty cycle
                x=0;
                if (PWM1 >=240)       // Setting max. DC as 240
                {
                PWM1=240;
                }
                }
                else if(stop==0)      // If stop key is pressed
                {
                x=1;
                PWM_Out=0;            // Clear the PWM output
                }
        }
}


void PWM_timer_Init (void) {          // Timer 0 used for PWM
```

```
        TMOD &= 0xF0;                    // Timer 0 mode setting
        TMOD |= 0x01;
        TL0 = 0x00;                      // Timer 0 reg. is cleared
        TH0 = 0x00;
        ET0 = 1;                         // Timer 0 interrupt enabled
        EA  = 1;                         // Enable global interrupt
        TR0 = 1;                         // Run timer0
}


void Timer0_ISR (void) interrupt 1      // Timer 0 ISR
{
        TR0 = 0;                         // Stop timer 0
        if (PWM_Out == 1 && x == 0)      // If PWM is on
        {
                PWM_Out = 0;             // Update the Duty cycle
                t = (255-PWM1) & 0xff;
                TL0 = t;
                TH0 = 0xFF;
        }
        else if (PWM_Out == 0 && x == 0)   // In PWM is off
        {
                PWM_Out = 1;             // PWM out is on
                t = PWM1 & 0xFF;         // Update the DC
                TL0 = 0xFF-t ;
                TH0 = 0xFF;
        }
        TF0 = 0;                         // Clear Timer 0 Flag
        TR0 = 1;                         // Run Timer 0
}
```

Experimental Result – Circuit Diagram:

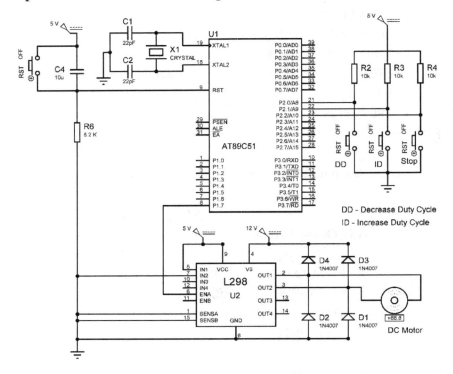

Conclusion:

The PWM signal is generated using timer 0 of 8051 microcontroller and the speed of DC motor has been controlled.

2.30	DIGITAL CLOCK USING LCD

Aim:

Write an Embedded C program for digital clock using the 8051 microcontroller and LCD.

Apparatus:

o   8051 Microcontroller kit and 16x2 LCD

Software Required:

o Keil μVision IDE / EdSim51DI Simulator/ any other supportive tool

Algorithm:

1. Declaration of ports for LCD
2. Declaration of functions
3. Clear the counter variables
4. Main function

    4.1 local variable declarations

    4.2 Initialize LCD for 8-bit and 2 lines mode

    4.3 Initialize timer 0 for 1 msec

    4.4 Write the hour, min and sec count values to LCD

    4.5 Repeat from step 4.4

5. Delay function for 1ms
6. Function to initialize timer 0 for 1ms
7. Function to write command to LCD
8. Function to write data to LCD
9. Function to display hour, min, sec values on LCD
10. ISR for Timer 0 – update the sec, min, and hour counter values

Embedded C Program:

```
#include<regx52.h>
sfr lcd = 0xa0;                     // Port 2 for LCD data bus
sbit rs =P3^0;                      // Port 3.0 for Register select
sbit e =P3^1;                       // Port 3.1 for Enable
void delay (unsigned int);          // function declarations
void InitTimer0 (void);
void lcd_command (unsigned int);
void lcd_data (unsigned char);
void DisplayLCD (unsigned int, unsigned int, unsigned int);

unsigned int msCount  = 0;          // global variable declarations
unsigned int secCount = 0;          // and initialization
unsigned int minCount = 0;
unsigned int hrCount  = 0;
```

```
void main(void)                           // main function
{
        unsigned int i;                   // local variable declarations
        unsigned char a[]={" Digital  Clock "};
        lcd_command(0x38);                // LCD initialization – 8-bit
        delay (5);                        // 2 –lines
        lcd_command(0x0e);
        delay (5);
        lcd_command(0x06);
        delay (5);
        lcd_command(0x01);    // clear screen
        delay (2);
        lcd_command(0x80);    // cursor at first line and first char
        delay (2);
        for (i=0;i<16;i++)
        {
        lcd_data(a[i]);       // display "Digital  Clock"
        delay (50);
        }

        InitTimer0();               // Initialize timer 0 for 1ms
        while(1)
        {
                if( msCount == 0 )      // display Hr:Min:sec
                {
                DisplayLCD(hrCount, minCount, secCount);
                }
        }
}


// subroutines
void delay(unsigned int t)        // delay function
{
  int u, v;
  for(u=0;u<t;u++)
  {
        for (v=0; v<123; v++);
        }
}
```

```
void InitTimer0(void)
{
        TH0=0xfc;                  // Timer register value for 1 ms
        TL0=0x66;
        TMOD=0x01;                 // Timer 0 – mode 1
        TF0 = 0;
        ET0 = 1;        // Enable Timer0 interrupts
        EA  = 1;        // Global interrupt enable
        TR0 = 1;        // Start Timer 0
}


void lcd_command(unsigned int c)        // write LCD command function
{
lcd=c;
rs=0;
e=1;
delay(1);
e=0;
delay(1);
}


void lcd_data(unsigned char d)          // write LCD data function
{
lcd=d;
rs=1;
e=1;
delay(1);
e=0;
delay(1);
}


// function for displays time in HH:MM:SS format
void DisplayLCD( unsigned int h, unsigned int m, unsigned int s )
{
        lcd_command(0xC4);                 // cursor position at C4
        delay (2);

        // Display Hour
        lcd_data( (h/10)+0x30 );                       // convert hour value into
```

```
        lcd_data( (h%10)+0x30 );          // ASCII for LCD

        //Display ':'
        lcd_data(':');

        //Display Minutes
        lcd_data( (m/10)+0x30 );          // convert minutes value into
        lcd_data( (m%10)+0x30 );          // ASCII for LCD

        //Display ':'
        lcd_data(':');

        //Display Seconds
        lcd_data( (s/10)+0x30 );          // convert seconds value into
        lcd_data( (s%10)+0x30 );          // ASCII for LCD
}

void Timer0_ISR (void) interrupt 1       // ISR for Timer 0
{
        msCount = msCount + 1;           // Count 1 msec

        if(msCount == 1000)              // 1000 msec means 1sec
        {
                secCount++;
                msCount=0;
        }

        if(secCount==60)                 // 60 sec means 1 minute
        {
                minCount++;
                secCount=0;
        }

        if(minCount==60)                 // 60 min means 1 hour
        {
                hrCount++;
                minCount=0;
        }
```

```
        if(hrCount==24)                 // if 24 hours reached,
        {
                hrCount = 0;             // clear hour count
        }

        InitTimer0();                    // initialize timer 0
}
```

Experimental Result – Circuit Diagram:

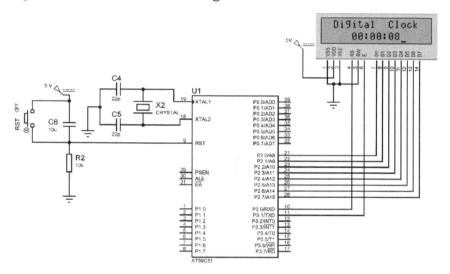

Conclusion:

The digital clock program has been executed in 8051 Microcontroller and clock time is displayed on the 16x2 LCD.

2.31	DISTANCE MEASUREMENT USING ULTRASONIC SENSOR

Aim:

Write an Embedded C program to measure the distance of target object using ultrasonic sensor and 8051 microcontroller.

Apparatus:

o   8051 Microcontroller kit, Ultrasonic sensor and 16x2 LCD

Software Required:

o   Keil µVision IDE / EdSim51DI Simulator/ any other supportive tool

Background:

HC-SR04 is an ultrasonic range sensor module designed to measure the distance between the sensor and target ranging from 2cm to 500cm. The sensor module sends a burst signal to the object, then picks up its echo and outputs a waveform whose time period is proportional to the distance. The microcontroller is used to perform necessary processing and displays the corresponding distance on the LCD. The HC-SR04 has four pins namely Vcc, Trigger, Echo, GND.

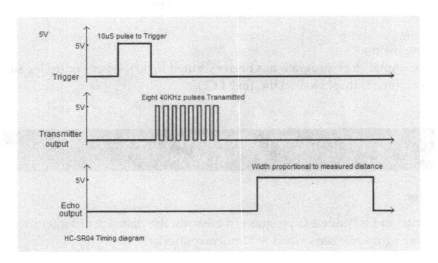

1) Vcc: 5V DC is connected to this pin.

2) Trigger: The trigger signal must be a pulse with 10uS ON time. Once the module receives a valid trigger signal, it generates 8 pulses of 40 kHz ultrasonic sound from the transmitter.

3) Echo: The status of this pin goes high when the module transmitted the pulses and it goes low when the receiver receives an echo signal from the target.

4) GND: Ground.

Working with Ultrasonic sensor step by step:

Step 1: Make the "Trig" pin of the sensor high for 10µs.

Step 2: 8 pulses of 40 kHz ultrasonic signal will be sent by the sensor, the Echo pin will go high.

Step 3: 40 kHz sound wave will bounce off the object and return to the sensor.

Step 4: When the sensor detects the reflected wave (Echo), the Echo pin will go low.

Step 5: The distance between target object and the sensor can be calculated from the length high status of the Echo pin.

Step 6: If there is no object, the Echo pin will stay high for 38 ms and then goes low.

Algorithm:

1. Declaration of ports for LCD
2. Declaration of ports for the ultrasonic sensor
3. Declaration of functions
4. Main function
   4.1 local variable declarations
   4.2 Function calls to initialize timers
   4.3 Function calls to initialize LCD
   4.4 Clear TimerCounter and Timer 1 registers
   4.5 Stop timer 1

4.6 Clear Trig pin and wait for sometimes

4.7 Set Trig pin and call 10us delay function

4.8 Clear Trig pin

4.9 Wait until echo =1

4.10 Start timer 1

4.11 Wait until echo =0

4.12 Stop timer 1

4.13 Calculate TimerCount value

4.14 Calculate distance value in cm

4.15 Display the distance value on the LCD screen

4.16 Repeat from step 4.4

5. Function to initialize timers

6. Function to initialize timer 0 for 1ms

7. Function to write command to LCD

8. Function to write data to LCD

9. Function to display hour, min, sec values on LCD

Embedded C Program:

```
#include<regx52.h>
#define dataport P2                 // Declaration of Ports for LCD
sbit rs = P3^0;
sbit rw = P3^1;
sbit e = P3^2;
sbit Trig= P1^7;                    // Declaration of P1.7 and P1.6
sbit Echo= P1^6;                    // for ultrasonic sensor

void init_timer();                  // function declarations
void init_lcd();
void delay_ms (unsigned int );
void delay_us ();
void lcddata(unsigned char);
void lcdcmd(unsigned int);

void main()                         // main function
{
unsigned long int TimerCount, dist;  // local variables
```

```
unsigned char d1, d2, d3;                    // declarations
init_timer();
init_lcd();

while(1)                    // forever loop
{
TimerCount =dist=0;         // clear variables
TH1=0x00; TL1=0x00;         // clear the timer 1 registers
TR1=0;                      // Turn-off timer 1
Trig=0;
delay_ms (10);
Trig=1;                     // 10us high pulse trigger
delay_us ();
Trig=0;
while(Echo==0);             // wait for sending 8 cycles of 40khz burst
TR1=1;
while(Echo==1);             // wait for echo to the sensor ( if target present)
TR1=0;

TimerCount = (TH1*256) + TL1;

// Ultrasonic Sound Velocity = 34029 (in cm per second)
// Timer gets incremented for every 1.085 us
// Distance in cm
```

$$= 34029*1.085*10^{-6}*\frac{TimerCount}{2} = 0.01846*TimerCount$$

```
dist = TimerCount * 0.01846;     // distance in cm
d1 = (dist/100) + 48;            // Sending distance value to LCD
d2 = ((dist%100)/10) + 48;
d3 = (dist%10) + 48;
lcdcmd(0xC9);  delay_ms(5);
lcddata(d1);   delay_ms(5);
lcdcmd(0xCA);  delay_ms(5);
lcddata(d2);   delay_ms(5);
lcdcmd(0xCB);  delay_ms(5);
lcddata(d3);   delay_ms(5);
}
}
```

```
// Subroutines
void init_timer() {
TMOD=0x11;                    // Initialize both timers in mode 1
TF0=0; TF1=0;
TR0 = 0; TR1 = 0;
}


void delay_ms (unsigned int msec)  // Function for delay in msec
{
unsigned int i;
        for(i=0; i<msec; i++) {
        TL0 = 0x66;
        TH0 = 0xFC;
        TF0 = 0;
        TR0 = 1;
        while (TF0 == 0);
        TR0 = 0;
        TF0 = 0;
        }
}


void delay_us ()                   // Function for us delay
{
        TL0 = 0xF5;
        TH0 = 0xFF;
        TF0 = 0;
        TR0 = 1;
        while (TF0 == 0);
        TR0 = 0;
        TF0 = 0;
}


void lcdcmd(unsigned int item)  //Function for sending CMD to LCD
{
        dataport = item;
        rs= 0;
        rw=0;
        e=1;
        delay_ms(2);
```

```
            e=0;
}


void lcddata(unsigned char item)  //Function for sending data to LCD
{
        dataport = item;
        rs= 1;
        rw=0;
        e=1;
        delay_ms(2);
        e=0;
}


void init_lcd()              // initialize LCD and display default characters
{
unsigned int i;
unsigned char a[]={"Distance of the "};     // default characters on LCD
unsigned char b[]={"Target =    cm "};

lcdcmd(0x38);              // for using 8-bit 2 row mode of LCD
delay_ms(2);
lcdcmd(0x0E);              // turn display ON for cursor blinking
delay_ms (2);
lcdcmd(0x06);              //display ON
delay_ms (2);
lcdcmd(0x01);              //clear screen
delay_ms (2);
lcdcmd(0x80);              // bring cursor to line 1
delay_ms (2);
for(i=0; i<16; i++)        // Write "Distance of the" on screen
{
lcddata(a[i]);
delay_ms (10);
}
lcdcmd(0xC0);              // bring cursor to line 2
delay_ms (2);
for(i=0; i<16; i++)        // Write "Target =    cm" on screen
{
lcddata(b[i]);
```

delay_ms (10);

}

}

Experimental Result – Circuit Diagram:

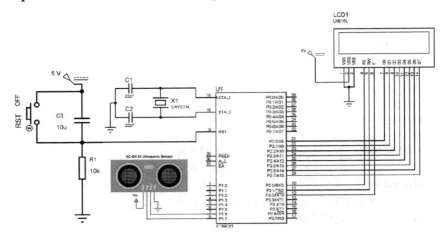

Conclusion:

The distance of the target has been measured using the 8051 Microcontroller and displayed it on 16x2 LCD.

2.32	SENDING SMS USING GSM SIM900

Aim:

Write an Embedded C program for sending SMS using GSM SIM900 and 8051 microcontroller.

Apparatus:

  o   8051 Microcontroller kit and GSM SIM900 module with SIM card

Software Required:

  o   Keil µVision IDE / EdSim51DI Simulator/ any other supportive tool

Background:

GSM (Global System for Mobile Communications) module is used to interact with the GSM network using a computer/MCU. GSM module only understands the AT commands. Some of them are,

- o AT+CSMS   – Select message service.
- o AT+CMGF   – Message format.
- o AT+CMGL   – List messages.
- o AT+CMGR   – Read the message.
- o AT+CMGS   – Send the message.
- o AT+CMGD   – Delete the message.
- o ATA   – Answer a call.
- o ATD   – Dial a number.
- o ATDL   – Dial the last outgoing number.
- o ATH   – Hang up the call.

GSM SIM900 is used for a GSM system that operates in 900 MHz. The 900 MHz band defined in the ETSI standard includes the primary GSM band (GSM-P) and the extension (E-GSM). The serial port of the microcontroller is used to communicate with the SIM900 module using PIN 10 (RXD) and 11 (TXD). The default baud rate of GSM SIM900 is 9600 bps.

Algorithm:

1. Declaration of port 1.7 for indication LED
2. Main function

   2.1 Turn-off LED

   2.2 Wait for 2 sec

   2.3 Test AT command with SIM900

   2.4 Send AT command to SIM900 for SMS message in Text Mode

   2.5 Send AT command to define the receiver's mobile number

   2.6 Send the message text to the serial port

   2.7 Send 0x1A for ctrl+z

   2.8 Send 0x0D and 0x0A for carriage return and line feed

   2.9 Turn-on LED

   2.10 Stop the program execution

3. Function to set the serial port in mode 1, 8-bit data, 1 stop bit, 1 start bit, receive on and run timer 1
4. Function for 1ms delay
5. Function to send serial data to SIM900
6. Function to send the string to SIM900

Embedded C Program:

```
#include<regx52.h>
sbit LED=P1^7;

void serialcomm()          // function to configure serial port for SIM900
{
TMOD=0x20;                         // Mode=2
TH1=0xfd;                          // 9600 baud
// Serial mode1, 8-Bit data, 1 Stop bit, 1 Start bit, Receive on
SCON=0x50;
TR1=1;                             // Start timer 1
}

void delay(unsigned int value)   // function for delay generation
{
    unsigned int i, j;
        for(i=0; i<value; i++)
        {
        for(j=0; j<123; j++);
        }
}

void serial_data(unsigned char x)     // function for sending serial data
{
SBUF=x;
while(TI==0);
TI=0;
}

void send_string (unsigned char *s)        // function for sending string
{
while(*s!=0x0)
```

```
{
SBUF=*s;
while(TI==0);
TI=0;
s++;
}
}

void main()                              // main function
{
LED = 0;
delay(2000);
serialcomm();                            // Configuring serial port

send_string ("AT\r\n");                  // AT Command Test
delay(2000);

send_string ("AT+CMGF=1\r\n");           // SMS message is set for Text Mode
delay(2000);

// Type receiver's mobile number - start with '0'
send_string ("AT+CMGS=\"09999999999\";\r\n");
delay(500);

send_string ("Hello World");    // SMS body
serial_data (0x1A);             // sends ctrl+z end of message in HEX
delay(500);

serial_data (0x0D);             // Carriage Return in Hex
serial_data (0x0A);             // Line feed in Hex
delay(2000);

send_string ("AT\r\n");
delay(2000);
```

LED =1;

while(1);

}

Experimental Result – Circuit Diagram:

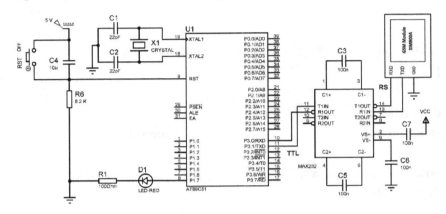

Conclusion:

The program for sending SMS using GSM SIM900 has been executed in 8051 Microcontroller.

2.33   MOTION DETECTION ALARM USING PIR SENSOR

Aim:

Write an Embedded C program for motion detection alarm system using PIR sensor and 8051 microcontroller.

Apparatus:

o   8051 Microcontroller kit, PIR sensor and Buzzer.

Software Required:

o   Keil μVision IDE / EdSim51DI Simulator/ any other supportive tool

Background:

PIR sensor detects infrared (IR) heat radiations. Usually, a living body emits infrared radiation. Therefore, the PIR sensor can be used to detect the presence of human beings. The PIR sensor having two slots and is connected to a differential amplifier. If a stationary object is present in front of the sensor, the two slots receive the same amount of radiation and the output is zero. If an object moving in front of the sensor, one of the slots receives more radiation than the other slot. This makes the output swing high or low. This change in output voltage is the result of the detection of motion.

PIR sensor has three pins:

1. GND: Power supply ground
2. VDD: +3.3-5 v power supply
3. Output: Digital output pin

Algorithm:

1. Declaration of port 2.7 for the buzzer
2. Declaration of port 1.4 for the PIR sensor
3. Declare the delay subroutine
4. Turn-off the buzzer
5. Check the state of PIR sensor

   If it is zero, turns-off the buzzer for 500 ms
6. Check the state of PIR sensor

   If it is one, turns-on the buzzer for 3000 ms
7. Repeat the steps from step 5
8. Develop the delay subroutine for 500 ms using FOR loop

Embedded C Program:

```
#include<regx51.h>
sbit buzzer = P2^7;              // declare P2.7 for buzzer
sbit PIR = P1^4;                 // declare P1.4 for PIR sensor
void delay(unsigned int);        // function declaration

void main()                      // main function
{
buzzer = 0;                      // Turn-off buzzer
while(1)                         // forever loop
{
        if (PIR == 0)            // If PIR = 0, Turn-off buzzer for 500 ms
        {
        buzzer = 0;
        delay (500);
        }
        else if (PIR == 1)       // If PIR =1, Turn-on buzzer for 3s
        {
        buzzer = 1;
        delay (3000);
        }
}
}

void delay(unsigned int x)       // function for delay generation
{
        unsigned int i, j;
        for(i=0; i<x; i++)
        {
        for(j=0; j<123; j++);
        }
}
```

Experimental Result – Circuit Diagram:

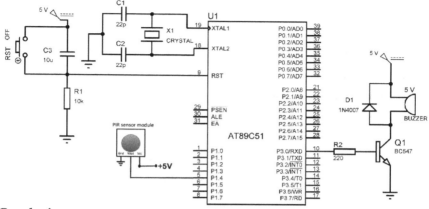

Conclusion:

The program for motion detection alarm using PIR sensor has been executed in 8051 Microcontroller.

2.34	WIRELESS CONTROLLED LED USING BLUETOOTH

Aim:

Write an Embedded C program to interface HC-05 Bluetooth module with the 8051 microcontroller and control the LED ON/OFF through Smartphone.

Apparatus:

o   8051 Microcontroller kit, HC-05 Bluetooth module, Smart Phone with Bluetooth Terminal App and an LED.

Software Required:

o   Keil µVision IDE / EdSim51DI Simulator/ any other supportive tool.

Background:

HC-05 is a Bluetooth module that is used for wireless communication. It works on universal asynchronous receiver transmitter

(UART) serial communication. The device can be operated in two modes; command mode and data mode.

- o The command mode is used for changing the settings of the Bluetooth module.
- o The data mode is used for data transfer between devices.

AT commands are required in command mode. The module works on 5V or 3.3V. It has six pins,

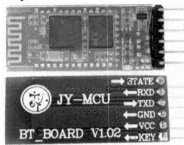

1. KEY : if set to HIGH, the module goes into command mode
2. Vcc : 5V supply
3. GND : Ground
4. TXD : TXD signal line
5. RXD : RXD signal line
6. State : Not connected

Step by step procedure:

- o Install a Bluetooth application in Smartphone from the play store.
- o After installation, pair the Bluetooth HC-05 module with Smartphone. The default pairing code is 1234.
- o Upload below program into the 8051 microcontroller.
- o From the Smartphone, turn ON the LED which is connected with MCU port by sending the character 'N' from the Bluetooth app and similarly turn OFF the LED by sending the character 'F' from the Bluetooth app.

Algorithm:

1. Declaration of port 1.5 for an LED
2. Main function

    2.1 Configure timer 1 in mode 2 and set the baud rate as 9600

    2.2 Receive the serial character and transmit the same to the serial port

    2.3 If the received char is 'N', turn-on the LED.

    2.4 If the received char is 'F', turn-off the LED.

3. The function definition for receive a serial character
4. The function definition for transmitting to a character to the serial port
5. The function definition for 1ms delay

Embedded C Program:

```
#include<regx52.h>
sbit LED = P1^5;
unsigned char x, y;             // Global variables declaration
void delay1ms (unsigned int) ;  //function declaration for 1ms delay
char rxdata(void);              //function for receiving a character
void txdata(unsigned char);     //function for sending a
void main(void)
 {
TMOD=0x20;          //timer 1, mode 2, auto reload
SCON=0x50;          // 8bit data, 1 stop bit, REN enabled
TH1=0xfd;           // timer value for 9600 baud rate
TR1=1;

while(1)            //repeat forever times
{
x = rxdata ();      //receive serial data from HC-05 module
txdata (x);         // transmit the received charater
        if(x=='N')  // if received char is 'N', turn-on the LED
        {
        LED = 1;
        delay1ms (500);     // wait for 500 ms
        }
        if(x=='F')  // if received char is 'F', turn-off the LED
        {
```

211

```
            LED = 0;
            delay1ms (500);          // wait for 500 ms
            }
            else
            {
            LED = LED;
            }
}
}

char rxdata ()
{
  while(RI==0);   // wait till RI becomes HIGH
  RI=0;           // make RI low
  y = SBUF;       // copy received data at y
  return y;       // return the received data to main function
}


void txdata(unsigned char z)
{
  SBUF = z;       // move data to be transmit on SBUF
  while(TI==0);   // wait till TI becomes high
  TI=0;           // clear TI
}
 void delay1ms (unsigned int t)        // 1ms timer delay
{
unsigned int i;
for(i=0;i<t; i++) {
THO=0xfc;                          // Timer register value for 1 ms
TL0=0x66;
TMOD=0x01;                         // Timer 0 – mode 1
TR0=1;                             // Start timer
while(TF0==0);                     // Wait until TF0 is set
TR0=0;                             // Stop timer0
TF0=0;                             // Clear Timer0 flag
}}
```

Experimental Result – Circuit Diagram:

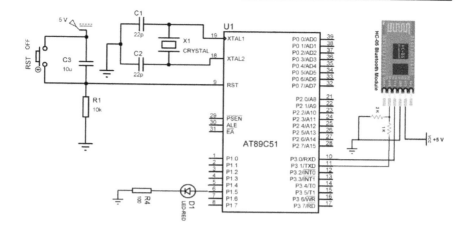

Conclusion:

Thus the HC-05 Bluetooth module has been interfaced with the 8051 microcontroller and controlled the LED using Smartphone.

*****

www.ingramcontent.com/pod-product-compliance
Lightning Source LLC
Chambersburg PA
CBHW071242050326
40690CB00011B/2232